A Sociology of English Religion

A Sociology of
English Religion

by

DAVID MARTIN

Lecturer in Sociology, London
School of Economics and Political Science

Introduction by D. G. MACRAE

Basic Books, Inc., Publishers
New York

CONTENTS

To my Parents

INTRODUCTION

QUITE simply this book is what it says. I hope as such it will be widely read and used both by that splendid Victorian creature, the general reader, who happily still survives and flourishes, and by the growing army of students of sociology and all who are practically concerned with the present state and future condition of faith in England. It is an accessible book, clear and unambiguous. It opens the gates to much wider prospects. It is also a tough-minded, quirky and very fast-moving book. This is what one would expect from its author and his place in the development of sociology in Britain. No one need agree with Dr Martin, but everyone, whether beginner in search of a brief textbook or general reader or scholar, will find much of value here.

The sociology of religion has developed late in Britain. Theology, the history of religions, comparative religion, ethnographic studies of religion, are all fields which the British have vigorously and successfully cultivated. But while, for example, political sociology has thoroughly established itself, it is only recently that sociologists have sympathetically concerned themselves with the investigation of religion, both belief and practice, in our society. Dr Bryan Wilson in Oxford and Dr John Highet were lonely pioneers in the 1950's. Today some of the best students, the most ingenious researchers, and the most interesting minds in British sociology concern themselves with the subject. The importance and fascination of the topic are sufficient to explain the present concern, altogether apart from the fact that no theory of society which does not take account of the religious component in culture is viable. What explains the past neglect?

One factor has been ideological and has operated in two ways. Religion has been thought of as a dying factor in an increasingly secular society. So future-directed a subject as sociology should not, therefore, be concerned with it. (Or religion has been dismissed as epiphenomenal: the surface appearance of harsh reality—a Freudian or Marxist illusion.) And in sociology there is always—as both virtue and vice—what Lord Annan has called the curious persistence of positivism; and positivism has either in its Comtean form offered a new religion, or more usually despised the non-natural and not thought it worth attention. These are real, if bad, reasons for neglecting a social reality so pervasive and powerful. In addition there has been at work among many sociologists—I nearly called them younger sociologists, but now they are often middle-aged—a very just and laudable desire to be concerned with learning from American sociology, so immensely rich and creative in the '40's and '50's. Unfortunately with few exceptions—Professor Talcott Parsons is one—American sociology of religion has been small in quantity and often sickly in quality. And lastly sociology—and funds for social research—has a bias towards the immediate and publicly accredited areas of social problems. Religion has not been seen as a field for applied sociological virtue.

Happily all, or nearly all, this is changing. The role of religion in society is accepted. The rise of terrible and of frivolous secular faiths characterizes our time. The persistence of faith and ritual is a fact, even in so irreligious and infidel a country as England. The permeation of our culture, the mediation of our social structure by religion cannot be ignored by the candid and intelligent student. It is true that a good deal of social surveying does ignore religion still: it is not intelligent. The very rise of political sociology has made neglect of the religious factor in party affiliation and voting behaviour, as well as in pressure-group formation, quite impossible.

Max Weber made much of the idea of a secular trend to the 'disenchantment' of the world as experienced in modern society. This 'demagicking' is a kind of fact, but I believe it has been misunderstood. There has been at work what I have elsewhere called a sort of 'wages-fund' theory of faith. But this is to neglect the capacity of men happily to believe many contradictory things at one time, to neglect the diversity of the roles we each play and which involve diverse items of social structure and cultural response, to neglect the infinite and unbounded nature of ideological space, and to misunderstand the truths about religion which are contained under the muddles of the Durkheimian analysis of the social roots of religion. In a world of innumerable idolatries—including the idolatry of positive science —the sociology of religion is a central concern, not a marginal indulgence.

Dr Martin brings acute learning and imagination to his theme. He brings also that scepticism of faith and commitment that he ascribes to Luther and Kierkegaard. It serves him well. And in addition he brings something which is, oddly, very near to being unique. This is a direct participation in and membership of English culture. Sociologists in England are often, like the present writer, members of minorities. This is helpful in some ways, for it gives a certain clarity and perspective, but it is not the only sociological virtue. Other sociologists have been or are very consciously self-made aliens, half-American in their character. Yet others are highly conscious proletarians—either by family origin, or self-made. Dr Martin may not be at ease in Sion, but he is certainly very much at ease in England. No one who was not could perhaps so readily see the continuities of belief and disbelief in our society, or the significance of progressiveness as faith, or understand so well the evidence of a specific music in English Christianity.

But that is quite enough. Dr Martin speaks for himself. The adventure of a sociology of English religion has begun, and this book both carries it further and makes it more comprehensible.

DONALD G. MACRAE,
Highgate, 26.ii.67

A*

MOTTO

'These proud Islanders . . . are never in earnest about anything that goes beyond palpable utility. Similarly they know nothing of religion, save that all preach devotion to ancient usages and defend its institutions, regarding them as a protection wisely cherished by the constitution against the natural enemy of the state.'

F. Schleiermacher
On Religion: speeches to its cultured despisers. First Speech: Defence

PREFACE

This book tries to cover a wide range of issues in a small space. Basically it is concerned with English (and Welsh) religious culture in a sense parallel to the studies by Rose, Runciman, Beer and McKenzie of English political culture. For a number of reasons, one of which is the meagre groundwork in the sphere of religion as compared with politics, it could not hope to rival those studies. This is why the last chapter provides a discursive indication of interesting areas for future research.

At the same time the discussion of religion in the world's first industrial country cannot help but raise profound queries, which I did not wish to avoid but which I could not hope to deal with at all adequately. The presence of these wider question marks causes the argument to oscillate between highly specific, even local, considerations, and the global issues encapsulated in the 'secularization thesis'. I hope it will be clear that I have reservations about that thesis, which is as contradictory as it is complicated. Broadly I am suspicious of it as a sociological or historical generalization about the current and future course of development, and also as a general prejudice against the institutional framework of religious awareness. Nevertheless 'secularization' has distinguished and persuasive proponents, notably Bryan Wilson in his *Religion in Secular Society*, which provides a sociological discussion in many ways complementary to the present work.

My reservations about 'secularization' do not mean that I have not found a great deal of stimulation from books like the Bishop of Woolwich's *The New Reformation?* or Harvey Cox's *The Secular City*, or that I reject all the liberations of thought and attitude which such books make explicit. But our perspectives must above all be realistic: to take but one example we need to be realistic when we consider ecumenical aspiration in relation to social fissures of nation, colour and status, and to the fundamental and very varied types of religious organization which had found constricted and creative lodgement within them. Theological discussion (like political discussion) must generally take place on a level of high-flown and self-deluding linguistic camouflage. Nevertheless the key word of recent debates has been honesty, and if we are to have the honesty about the Church—that 'wonderful and sacred mystery' as the prayer book very properly calls it—then sociological perspectives and research are not a marginal luxury but an essential.

DAVID MARTIN

London School of Economics
and Political Science 1966

ACKNOWLEDGEMENTS:
PUBLIC AND PRIVATE

I AM grateful to Margaret Stacey and the Clarendon Press for permission to utilize material from *Tradition and Change: a Study of Banbury*. Mass Observation have kindly allowed me to quote from *Puzzled People*, and the Gallup Poll have let me forage in their files as well as basing many observations on the publication *Television and Religion* sponsored by ABC Television.

I am also grateful to Professor Donald MacRae for various comments, and for the broad suggestions on the subject of 'secularization' which made the viewpoint of this book easier to achieve.

The Rev. David Edwards, Dean of King's College, Cambridge, was initially responsible for suggesting that I should write about this particular subject. The Rev. John Bowden of the SCM Press made the whole process of production very pleasant, and Miss Jean Cunningham tactfully curbed my worst solecisms; such remnants of sociologists' English as remain are, I hope, minimal and necessary. I also derived a great deal of help from those who kindly responded to requests in the press for information—even those who expressed the hope that I would deal with true religion rather than false.

My major personal debt is to my wife, who has heard it all before and who tried to prevent me from indulging prejudices more than was necessary for my psychological well-being. The liveliness and acerbity of those prejudices may suggest another debt. A pigeon put among the cats is not in a position of maximum security. The London School of Economics is hardly renowned for piety, and a believer working with a noble company of 'cultured despisers' needs frequently to remind himself that faith, in Luther's and Kierkegaard's sense, involves a vigorous scepticism not only about the Church but about all those quasi-religious props that contemporary men (cultured and otherwise) use to maintain their sanity—occasionally with regrettable success.

CHAPTER ONE

Historical Background:
Dissenters and Abstainers

MOST people suppose that our comparative indifference to religious practice nowadays has its first roots in the effects of the industrial revolution. Substantially they are right.

Yet the evidence is conflicting. Rural societies are not necessarily given to unanimous practice, as many areas of disaffection in nineteenth-century France show, and we know that the overgrown bulk of London harboured indifference as well as heresy even in the 'religious' seventeenth century. Indeed the historian Christopher Hill has suggested that in the seventeenth century the very lowest social strata were largely outside both Church and Dissent.

We find further references to disaffection from organized religion in the post-Restoration period and the eighteenth century: in certain remote areas like Cornwall and Wales, later to be evangelized by the Methodists or other nonconformists, in such pockets of industrialism as were already appearing (the Kingswood miners for example), and in the back streets of London. We need only to look at Hogarth to appreciate both the brutalized life of the London slums and the literally somnolent piety of the churches. The picture here is a long way from the orderly rural world of a squire like Sir Roger de Coverley, presiding over a rural congregation as it devoutly attended the patient homilies of Archbishop Tillotson.

Of course, these comments partly concern the quantity of practice, partly its quality, and they probably reflect a rather gloomy nonconformist view of the ecclesiastical world before

Wesley.[1] Recent demographic research as well as recent ecclesiastical history has tried to improve the image of eighteenth-century Anglicanism. So far as formal adherence and belief is concerned Peter Laslett has gone so far as to suggest that our ancestors were literal Christian believers, unanimous in their practice.[2] Yet his own evidence is at odds with his argument. He records an instance where some 200 out of 401 villagers made their Easter communion, a number which dropped to 125 with no comparable drop in population. He even mentions 'much smaller attendances' in other places.

From these uncertainties about abstention we turn to Dissent. Something perhaps needs to be said about the broader background of dissenting religion. In most of the nonconforming bodies we can trace a process whereby they have evangelized a segment of the less prestigious social strata (usually not the very lowest) and have then lifted this segment to a higher position on the social scale. This process has sometimes emasculated their capacity to repeat the task of evangelization, so that a new group has been needed to repeat the process a second and third time. Thus the Salvation Army partly took over from the Methodists and the Pentecostalists from the Salvation Army. A correlative process has involved a cooling of religious zeal and an intrusion of formality, perhaps even of high culture.

This pattern, in part, fits Dissent at the onset of the industrial revolution. Actually the older dissenting bodies of the seventeenth century, who either left or were ejected from the Establishment extended their social range not only downwards but also very high in the scale, and were in some cases closely identified with high culture. But at any rate it is true that such considerable contacts as they originally had with lower strata weakened as the effects of thrift and discipline brought them success in this life as well as salvation in the world to come. They

[1] Cf. J. H. Whiteley, *Wesley's England*, Epworth, 1938. The view of recent nonconformist scholarship can be found in R. Davies and E. G. Rupp, *A History of the Methodist Church in England*, Epworth, 1965, vol. 1, esp. Introduction and ch. 1.

[2] P. Laslett, *The World We Have Lost*, University Paperbacks, 1965. Research is currently proceeding which will throw light on this question. Dr Wrigley, Reader in Demography at Cambridge, who is associated with this research, suggests that at the moment we do not really know the facts, although there was evidently considerable variation according to the character of the incumbent.

were particularly successful in business. Moreover, the fact that they were excluded from the ancient universities, with their ossified curricula, forced them back on lively academies which produced many notable innovators, in science, in technology and in commerce.[3]

So it was that these dissenting bodies, some of whom had partly initiated and partly succumbed to rationalism and to theological liberalization, were amongst the ideological and psychological catalysts required for the take-off period of England's industrial revolution. When that take-off occurred it fused with a quite new development of Dissent: the Methodist revival.[4] Of course, the very word 'Methodism' links the new dissenters with the old, and their devotion to method has led some historians to suggest that where the older bodies helped initiate industrialism the newer bodies provided the factory system with a work discipline, as well as affording a warm refuge from bleak reality. However the Methodists differed from the seventeenth-century Puritans in that the millenarianism which broke out so widely under the stimulus of the Civil War only recurred in a few small sects, like the Southcottians. Moreover in the early phases of Methodism the vigorous political radicalism of seventeenth-century groups such as the Levellers only reproduced itself in rather minor manifestations like the Kilhamites. Yet the Methodists, if they administered a much slighter shock to the social structure and if they reached less high in the scale than classical Puritanism (the Countess of Huntingdon and her circle apart) spread wider and deeper than previous nonconformity.[5]

Methodism indeed has frequently been given the credit for the absence of bloody revolution in Britain. How far this may be judged to have been deserved depends partly on whether the reference is to members or to numbers influenced, but either way it seems that the power of the revival was not great enough to be

[3] E. E. Hagen, *On the Theory of Social Change*, Dorsey Press, 1962.

[4] Interesting Marxist accounts of early Methodism may be found in E. P. Thompson, *The Making of the English Working Class*, Gollancz, 1963, and E. J. Hobsbawm, *Labouring Men*, Weidenfeld and Nicolson, 1964, and *Primitive Rebels*, Manchester University Press, 1959. The account by Thompson is not friendly in tone.

[5] W. J. Warner, *The Wesleyan Movement in the Industrial Revolution*, Longmans, 1930.

regarded as the sole cause of this result. What is certainly true is that when the frights of the Napoleonic period were over, Methodism gradually shifted to the side of the nascent Liberal Party, and that the same qualities of discipline (if not of innovation) which had raised the old dissenter in the social scale now performed the same service for some of the Methodists. By the mid-century the chapels of the industrial revolution confronted the church of the rural squirearchy numerically, politically and socially.[6]

But together chapels and church alike faced a massive abstention from religious observance in large areas of the new cities. Manchester was the first of these to excite the wonder and the horror of the world, and it was followed by Birmingham, soon to be presided over by Unitarian and other dissenting commercial dynasties culminating in Joseph Chamberlain. We need to remember that the 'unchurched masses' of these places were now physically separated from the pious middle classes, whereas in the eighteenth century, in districts like Chelsea for example, the two groups had lived in close proximity. Such concentrations of the 'dangerous and perishing classes' aroused both Christian and political concern.

Thus the Church of England was concerned about the growth of the dissenting chapels, and people of all religious persuasions were concerned about the large-scale abstention from practice in the bigger urban centres. As Engels had pointed out in 1845 'the workers are not religious and do not attend church'. Religion and churchgoing are not in fact identical, but Engels' statement embodied a substantial truth. Other writers referred to a 'spiritual vacuum' in the industrial cities. Hence in 1851, for the first (and only) time, it was proposed to include religious practice in the arrangements for the decennial census. The chapels hoped to utilize the results for propaganda against establishment and many churchmen were reluctant to co-operate for that very reason, except that non-co-operation only diminished the chances of the Established Church showing up well numerically. Both sides to a somewhat heated debate realized that any results

---

[6] This process is documented in E. R. Taylor, *Methodism and Politics, 1791-1851*, Cambridge University Press, 1935.

would at least spotlight the need for new efforts and strategies in the industrial areas.

The Religious Census of 1851 is the central piece of evidence about mid-nineteenth-century religious practice, but it deserves to be interpreted with more than usual caution. Certainly the formulae used by its main interpreter, Horace Mann, favoured the Church of England by the weighting given to morning as against evening attendances; and the figures for Roman Catholics are also probably an underestimate. We have also to remember that the high proportion of those considered non-eligible is partly accounted for by the youthfulness of the population.

According to a study carried out by William Pickering it seems that some 7 million persons attended church on the chosen day. This was about 36% of the total population and can be divided almost equally between Anglicans and Nonconformists with the Roman Catholics accounting for a mere 4% of worshippers. Hence the result showed the main rivals almost level,[7] with the small Protestant sects, even the vigorous Mormons, making comparatively little impact and the Catholics not yet a major force.

It showed more. Taking all denominations together attendance of persons by counties ranged between 57% and 21%, with Bedford and Huntingdon at the head and (in descending order) Surrey, Middlesex, Northumberland, Durham, Lancashire, Cumberland and London at the foot. Of course percentages compiled in this way permit only the crudest comparisons, but at least some pattern emerges. Wales as a whole was distinguished by high attendance. The crucial statistics were those showing a very high correlation between proportion of attendance and size of town: the larger the town, the lower the proportion. Such figures did indeed illuminate the 'spiritual destitution' of the great cities.

Examination by districts within cities suggests that it was not

[7] W. S. F. Pickering, 'The Religious Census of 1851—a useless experiment?' (with maps), *British Journal of Sociology* 18, 1967. Dr Pickering makes very clear the complications involved, and to understand these the reader should really consult his careful and exhaustive work. Another useful source is K. S. Inglis, 'Patterns of Worship in 1851', *Journal of Ecclesiastical History* 11 (1), 1960, pp. 74-86.

so much the factor of size in itself which required attention as the distribution of classes, their conditions and divergent ways of life. Research recently done in Bristol, for example, a city with an unusually high attendance, indicates a variation from area to area which illustrates the rule that the lower the socio-economic class the more attenuated the practice.[8]

Nonconformity and Roman Catholicism require further discussion since they have both been credited with a greater ability to maintain themselves in the new urban areas than Anglicanism. If we consider first the nonconformists we need to be careful about which group we have in mind: the role of Primitive Methodists and Baptists for example still awaits full examination, especially an assessment period by period and area by area. That nonconformity was *relatively* more successful in the northern towns than Anglicanism is clear enough. By comparison Anglican strength lay in the middle rural counties between Dorset and the Wash and in the far West Midlands. But if we look at the evidence of the Rev. Dr Abraham Hume in his pamphlet *The Church of England the Home Missionary to the Poor, especially in our large towns* (1862) and at Tindall's *Wesleyan Methodist Atlas* (1873) some contrary tendencies are also evident.[9]

Hume's argument was designed to show that the 'voluntary system' leads dissenters to rely on local resources and therefore to gravitate *away* from the poorer areas. Whether or not his attacks on voluntaryism follow from his evidence (which is at its most detailed for Liverpool) the tendency for dissenters to move 'up the hill' literally and socially is attested from plenty of sources. Edward Miall, editor of *The Nonconformist*, himself mentions it as a characteristic item of abuse from supporters of the Establishment. Sobriety, discipline and mutual aid had their natural consequences, and the nonconformists could hardly avoid a degree of social mobility.

Dr Hume also argues that in 'dens of vice' the only chapels are secularist or Mormon. He then documents this by a comparative

[8] Research undertaken by R. M. Goodrich.
[9] E. H. Tindall, *The Wesleyan Methodist Atlas of England and Wales*, 1873, and A. Hume, *Remarks on the Census of Religious Worship*, 1860, and *The Church of England the Home Missionary to the Poor . . .* , 1862.

study of districts based on the population totals relative to each dissenting chapel. He compares districts within England and Wales as a whole, and then districts within London and within Wales. Over the whole country he found dissenting provision poorest in Middlesex, Surrey, Lancashire, Warwickshire, Sussex and Kent, and most comprehensive in North Wales, the North Riding, Cornwall, South Wales and Lincoln. This at least shows the weakness of Dissent in the south-east and in the western penumbra of London, as well as its power in the Celtic fringes. Clearly it was not strong in the two counties embracing Liverpool, Manchester and Birmingham.

Within London itself Hume finds the best provision of chapels in Hackney, Wandsworth, Hampstead and Lewisham, and the worst in Hanover Square, West London, St Giles and Strand. Nobody would raise an eyebrow at the scarcity of dissenters in the richest areas of the capital but Hume is chiefly anxious to show that they are almost equally weak in the very poor districts of St Giles and Strand. Similarly, within Wales he finds them weakest in the new industrial areas, Swansea, Merthyr Tydfil and Neath, and strongest in the northern fastnesses of Dolgelly, Llanfyllin and Bala. This, however, is unfair since they were nevertheless still very strong in industrial South Wales. Dr Hume concludes triumphantly that dissenting provision is 53 times as comprehensive in the best districts of Wales as in the worst of London.

Of course, Hume is tendentious but not substantially inaccurate. Tindall's *Wesleyan Methodist Atlas* shows for example that there were 500 seats available in Chorlton-cum-Hardy (pop. 1,466) and only an equal number available in Ardwick (pop. 28,066), an area in the centre of Manchester. He shows on the one hand the strong superiority of Methodist increase over population increase during the century (in spite of mid-century dissension and fission) but he indicates that even at that time there was relatively greater success in the suburbs and the country.[10] If we accept a suggestion by Inglis there was also greater success in the small towns, where relations between

---

[10] Quoted by B. E. Jones in 'Sociology and the Work of the Ministry', *London Quarterly and Holborn Review*, Jan. 1963.

master and man had not yet become fully depersonalized.[11] The great name of Methodism in the first half of the nineteenth century, Jabez Bunting, had himself made the point about the country and had called upon Methodists to remember they were essentially 'a rural connection'. At any rate Methodism became the only substantial form of rural Dissent, outside the south Midlands and Wales. One has only to read the fine account given of local rural Methodism in M. K. Ashby's *Joseph Ashby of Tysoe* to gain an idea of its relation to the conflicts of the time. It was after all a Methodist preacher, Joseph Arch, who was the moving spirit in the abortive agricultural labourers' union.

The other religious force credited with some ability to retain working-class allegiance was Roman Catholicism. It may be useful to begin by summarizing the territorial, numerical and social position of Catholicism in Ireland. Again we turn to Dr Hume, and his commentary on the Irish Census of 1861.[12] This, of course, is after the great dispersion in the late 1840's but there is no reason to think the balance of forces by area and by class substantially different from twenty years previous.

Four out of five Irishmen were Roman Catholics: they were strongest in the south-west, weakest in the north-east. Presbyterians were sharply concentrated in the north-east, while Anglicans formed a weaker belt between the Presbyterians and the Catholics and were somewhat more evenly spread altogether. Dr Hume's main object is to show that with each step up the scale in the direction of honorific and socially useful occupations (health, education, science, art, justice, property and banking) the Protestant proportion increases, until with the Lord-Lieutenancy they were represented 100%. Roman Catholics were most over-represented amongst 'labourers, miscellaneous dealers, shopkeepers and assistants unspecified, prisoners and beggars', and Protestants most over-represented amongst 'vitriol rectifiers, knights, plate-makers, gun-cartridge makers and Russia merchants'.

Such, roughly was the social character of the starving and

[11] K. S. Inglis, *Churches and the Working Classes in Victorian England*, Routledge, 1963.
[12] A Hume, *Results of the Irish Census of 1861*, Rivingtons, 1864.

largely Catholic population which arrived in England during the 'forties and the 'fifties, somewhat indeed to the distaste of their English co-religionists. How then did they fare in England during the following half-century?

For a general account we have John Jackson's *The Irish in Britain*, but we are here largely concerned with the religious side of the new settlement and with the general situation of Catholicism. Anthony Spencer has described that situation as basically comprising a stream of English Catholics, a trickle of converts and a flood of Irish. The trickle of converts was important only insofar as it helped expand a minute Catholic middle class. The Irish peasants however had now stepped into precisely those places in an expanding industrial economy which the English were not unhappy to vacate: the railway navvies, the dockers, the builders, the street traders—and the soldiers. The flood was not continuous throughout the century: after the 1850's it levelled off until the second major influx almost a hundred years later, and the slow pace of Catholic expansion reflected this: 5% in 1851 and 6.5% in 1911.[13]

A concentration of Irish in these sectors of economy meant that the Roman Catholic Church experienced the usual forces of erosion, but armed it with certain advantages. The priesthood, so far as it was Irish, was associated with the long struggle against English exploitation, and came from the same exploited groups. It was distinguished only by its priestly status and by comparative education, both of which enabled it to act as guardian to the immigrant community. On the other hand the English priesthood acted as a repellent. But the Catholic Church was also simply the only vehicle of ethnic identity (just as *all* churches were in the American situation); and the concentration in particular areas of large towns outweighed the disadvantages of inadequate facilities. Indeed these facilities were frequently provided by Irish publicans, who gave their parlours to the Mass and their sons to the priesthood. Lapsing certainly occurred, and on a considerable scale if we compare expected with actual Catholic population, even allowing for the appalling death-rate which

[13] I lean here on material in A. E. C. W. Spencer, 'The Demography and Sociography of the Catholic Community in England and Wales', *Downside Symposium*, 1965.

the community experienced. Probably lapsing was most marked
in the second and third generations of immigrants. Moreover
certain groups, like the railway navvies, who included many
Irish, became notorious for irreligion.

To some extent the Catholics increasingly provided a mirror
image of native nonconformity. The nonconformists were socially mobile and particularly strong amongst tradespeople; the
Catholics were somewhat more static and especially weak in the
trading population. The nonconformists were strong in the north-
east, south-west and Wales, whereas the Catholics were strong in
the north-west, especially Lancashire, and in London. Catholics
were numerous in the great urban centres and only gradually
spilled over from their 'reception areas', while nonconformists
were to be found in the country, the small towns and the suburbs.
Hostile observers even commented that one group was over-
represented in the gaols while the other was under-represented.
Thus socially, regionally and in terms of type of area the two
confessions contrasted one with another.

Let us now try to summarize the situation as it existed in the
second half of the nineteenth century. Above all it was a period
of religious boom for the middle classes.[14] These classes were now
at the height of their power and like the contemporary American
middle classes not exactly suffering from those deprivations frequently cited as spurs to piety. Yet it is from evidence which they
provide that we conclude the period was one of doubt and
anxiety.[15] This is partly because we derive our impressions from
literary sources, which are as likely to overemphasize the nodal
points of doubt as they are to misrepresent the impact of neo-
Catholicism. We need to remember that the intellectual struggles
of a George Eliot or the sad premonitions of a Matthew Arnold
affected only the tiniest of minorities. And even amongst these
one can trace either a Puritan psychology or some persistent
attempt to transmute faith into a viable form such as one finds

[14] According to E. R. Wickham in *Church and People in an Industrial City*,
Lutterworth, 1957.
    For historians' views on this period see G. Kitson Clark, *The Making of
Victorian England*, Methuen, 1962, and R. C. K. Ensor *England 1870-1914*,
Clarendon Press, 1936.
    [15] A good study of doubt, anxiety, etc., is W. E. Houghton, *The Victorian
Frame of Mind*, Yale University Press, 1957.

in T. H. Green.[16] Even the aristocracy, we may suppose, not notorious for righteousness, accommodated itself to the piety of the court, although the contrast between the wayward morals of Palmerston and the vigorous bourgeois rectitude of Gladstone is clear enough.

The argument is not that churchgoing was solely middle-class: after all on most criteria that grouping accounts for a mere 10 to 20% even today. One is merely indicating the existence of alienation in the massed slums. Moreover this alienation was not at all gradual, nor can it be blamed on to the impact of universal education after 1870: it derived simply and almost immediately from the urban structure consequent on large-scale industrialization.[17] No one denies that for the rest—the tradesmen, the growing army of clerks, the vast number of domestic servants, those employed in some situation of retainer status or personal deference, and the diminishing rural populations—churchgoing remained the normal habit.

And yet the English working class was rarely secularist, and even such small pockets of secularism as appeared diminished towards the end of the century.[18] The so-called 'Labour Churches' maintained only a very tenuous existence.[19] Nor was the working class politically radical, in spite of the exceptions documented by Edward Thompson and Royden Harrison: then, as now, it was equally impervious to organized radical politics and to organized religion.

Not quite impervious. The extractive industries, mining and fishing, seemed capable of harbouring both religious and political radicalism. Fishermen in the north-east of Scotland might become puritanical Brethren or in Devon might respond to Primi-

[16] M. Richter, *The Politics of Conscience*, Weidenfeld and Nicolson, 1965, has considerable material on the religious mutations of this period, as well as on the 'socialization' of evangelical humanitarianism and on the settlement movement. It is useful to read this in conjunction with K. Heasman's *Evangelicals in Action*, Bles, 1962.

[17] I follow here K. S. Inglis, *op. cit.*, and E. R. Wickham, *op. cit.*

[18] Cf. J. Eros, 'The Rise of Organized Free Thought in Mid-Victorian England', *Sociological Review* 2 (1), July 1954. Interesting work is currently being done on aspects of nineteenth-century secularism by E. Royle of Christ's College, Cambridge.

[19] There is a useful chapter on the Labour Churches in E. J. Hobsbawm, *Primitive Rebels*.

tive or Wesleyan Methodism. Perhaps the miners were the more capable of eventually breaking out into the politics of the extreme left: in the Rhondda Valley and West Fife for example.

It may be important that one is speaking primarily of an *English* working class for whom a pattern was set early on in the industrial revolution. Some of the areas to develop later, often with alien populations and experiencing the impact of a developed capitalism and more sophisticated ideas, showed tendencies more characteristic of the Continent. For example, in the west of Scotland a partly Irish and immigrant population developed a semi-brutalized culture very different from that of industrial Lancashire which eventually exploded in the Clydeside 'Revolutionaries' and several varieties of Marxist sectarianism.

Finally, we turn to London at the very end of this period for a more detailed exemplification of the tendencies so far described. London was twice the object of full-scale statistical surveys quite apart from the qualitative assessment of Charles Booth. The surveys by the *British Weekly* in 1886 and the *Daily News* in 1903 showed roughly the same picture. The 1903 *Daily News* report as presented by Mudie-Smith and his collaborators is worth some more extended summary.[20]

It was reckoned that in inner London, of persons of seventeen and over, one out of three of those who could attend church did so: in outer London one out of two. Out of the total population of inner and outer London, some 6¼ millions, nearly 1¼ millions attended: one in five. Of these the nonconformists and the Church of England accounted for about half a million each. Roman Catholics numbered nearly 100,000 and 'others' some 72,000. 'Others' included about 12,000 (male) Jews, many of them recently arrived from Eastern Europe during the Diaspora of the 1890's.

When the totals were compared with the previous *British Weekly* it was found that whereas the Free Churches were almost holding their ground in relation to increased population the Church of England had declined sharply, a decline which in-

[20] R. Mudie Smith (ed.), *The Religious Life of London*, Hodder and Stoughton, 1904. See Michael Jackson's summary of Charles Booth in *Theology* 64, Nov. 1961.

cluded all social classes. The Baptists had advanced notably,
and the Wesleyan Forward Movement, with its emphasis on central Missions with a strong social concern, had held ground which
would otherwise have been lost if the older circuit system had
been relied upon alone.

The compilers of the survey were remarkably clear about
which groups and which areas were disaffected from organized
Christianity: and they pointed out there was an almost uniform
connection between socio-economic class and churchgoing, so
that certain areas only retained such minuscule totals as they did
by virtue of the tradesmen or the middle-class enclaves still
remaining within them. Soon these islands would be submerged
by the universal flight to the suburbs. It was in these suburbs
that the ambitious clerk and 'self-centred business man' provided
pillars of the churches. The survey was also clear about the existence of a class below the working class, living in total misery,
'dead under a mound of social injustice', and almost completely
alienated from the churches. These people had not even the
energy to display the political radicalism or the occasional
secularism of the artisanate.

What degree of penetration occurred across these lines of
class? Only the Sunday Schools had any substantial success,
and this would have occurred, it was said, even if the teachers
had been 'mild-mannered Buddhists', provided at least they were
white. Free Churchmen very rarely touched the submerged
tenth: characteristically they were the 'social aristocracy' of the
poorer boroughs (too comfortable to be Anglicans, as one observer put it) or the employees of large business houses lately up
from the provinces. The Salvation Army certainly went into the
poorest regions but it possessed remarkably few members, although many used its social agencies and some converts were
perhaps 'passed on' to the more conventional churches. The
sects, and groups like the Primitive Methodists, made some
marginal impact on the poor.

It was often supposed that 'ritualism' had some success in the
working classes. True, the Roman Catholics were described as
strong among illiterate Irish and Italians (as well as amongst
'rich visitors on Highgate Hill'). But what of the effects of Anglo-
Catholicism? This movement was now strong in the diocese

of London and some Anglo-Catholic priests actually espoused socialist opinions. Some must have been cast in the mould of the heroic Father Dolling; others one fears may have resembled a certain Dr Lee: neither were very successful. One cannot resist quoting Dr Lee's own analysis of the situation, since it illustrates only too well one aspect of the ritualistic temper: he regarded the current situation as due to '(1) Atheistic Board [State] Schools. (2) Destruction of the parochial system, by which people became independent choosers rather than learners. (3) Mischievous influence of Dissent. (4) Co-operation in philanthropic work with agnostics, atheists, etc. (5) Preaching in music halls and theatres, which destroys reverence and fosters sensationalism.'[21]

The Mudie-Smith team distinguished sharply between the great spreading central area of 'grey' and the suburbs: we may perhaps interpolate an elaboration of this notion which appeared somewhat earlier, in the *Record* article just quoted. This points to a series of concentric circles or 'lines' stemming from the centre. Firstly there was the riverside railway area, where the very poorest lived, together with many criminals. Second there was the 1818-1884 region: once professional but now fallen and tenanted largely by artisans and small shopkeepers. Third, there was an area of superior clerks and small merchants, not yet let out, but already in process of falling socially. With each movement into the inner, most dejected, areas the influence of the churches was so much the less.[22]

Nobody could suppose this failure was due to lack of trying. The story of Christianity in London at this period is one of extraordinary activity and heroic overwork on the part of Evangelicals and ritualists alike. The surveyors had their own explanations however for the small impact of so much devotion, money and effort.[23]

Partly it was put down to the cultural gap and lack of communication: either the mysterious evangelical language of Canaan or the even more mysterious and frigid Anglican ritual.

[21] Article entitled 'South London: its Religious Condition, its Needs and its Hopes', in *The Record* (the Southwark Diocesan Magazine), 6 Jan. 1888.
[22] *Ibid.*
[23] Most of these explanations can be found in Charles Masterman's essay in Mudie Smith, *op. cit.*

The disunity of the churches was also to blame, and their moral failures, for example, the failure to give working men positions of status and responsibility, the constant dispensation of a flood of charity instead of social justice, the 'people be good' attitude of Anglicanism and the indifferent business Christians of the suburbs. On the other side there was the sheer apathy of the poor and the embarrassment which their poverty brought them on entering church.

But the weight of explanation lay most heavily on the problem of uprooting from the countryside, the breaking of old attachments and assimilation to a pre-existing majority pattern. In any case the working-class Sunday needed to be the one moment of respite from the grind: a nap, a newspaper, a saunter, an early supper and a pipe. And Sunday was also the great day for visiting by shop assistants, clerks and warehousemen, who settled down to play games and give concerts in their tiny parlours. Moreover, visiting equally affected the rich, and amongst them a new important source of infidelity had made its appearance: the weekend habit.

APPENDIX

Charles Booth on 'Religion in London in relation to Class'[24]

There are some amongst the oldest of English families whose traditions hold them faithful to the Church of Rome, but with these and a few other exceptions of less importance, the great bulk of those of rank and station amongst our people belong to the Church of England, and their relations with the Church are easy and confident. They are not only steady supporters, but for the most part, truly and warmly attached members. For them the union of Church and State is more than a phrase. Both in town and country they and their families attend the services of the Church; many of their women devote their lives to Church work, while from their men have come large numbers of clergy and some of the greatest of religious philanthropists. Their

[24] *Life and Labour of the People in London:* Third Series, *Religious Influences*, Macmillan, 1902, vol. 7, ch. 10, § 1.

devotional expression is, as a rule, cold and unemotional, but with no class is religion more completely identified with duty. They belong to all branches of the Church: High or Low, or what may perhaps be called 'Central', and ask, as a rule, no further licence. Doctrinal difficulties do not trouble them much; their balance is not easily upset. The same mental as well as social position is occupied, and the same course pursued from generation to generation, handed down from father to son, and from mother to daughter. All their traditions are conservative. The part played by religion in their lives is as a rule by no means large but it is constant.

Those who come next in the social scale, who fill the principal places in the Civil Service, officer the Army and Navy, and plead in our courts of law, are also mostly members of the Church of England, and supply the Church with many of her clergy. Amongst this class religious observance is usual, but the attitude towards religion is perhaps less calm than that described above, it may be because less simply connected with duty. With these people religious feeling when it arises is very likely to take the shape of reaction and revolt from the stress of worldly existence, which is otherwise apt to be the law of their being, and then they, and especially the women, fling themselves into good works, or rush into extremes of religious doctrines and practices. There are among them many restless minds and lives with no safe anchorage; and it is the troubled condition of such souls, more than anything else, that has given rise to the wild hopes of Rome for the conversion of England, and to the dreams of others who live in expectation of a new spiritual dispensation, accompanied by strange credulities and dabblings in mediaeval magic.

The borders of this class have been extended by increase of wealth, but the new comers have by the very law of their advancement shared to the full in the stress of worldly life, and in the characteristics it produces both with men and women. If belonging previously to some religious denomination outside the Establishment, they have usually left it behind them and joined the Church of England; but it is much to be wished that with the general rise in social status of the Nonconformist bodies, this unsatisfactory form of conventional development may come to an end; and of this change there are now some hopeful signs.

With the next social layer, consisting of legal and other professional men, some civil servants, men of business, wholesale traders and large retailers, the Nonconformist bodies—Presbyterians, Congregationalists and Wesleyans, with Unitarians and the Society of Friends, and a few of the Baptist congregations which can lay claim to social standing—take the lead of the Church of England. Class position amongst the Nonconformists goes very much by congregations, the worshippers sorting themselves in this way much more than do those who attend the parish churches. Amongst these people those of highest social grade share in the worldly striving and push of the class above, but their religious anchorage, with the Nonconformists at least, is likely to be more secure. The place of religion in their lives is fully recognized. If they succeed they give thanks to God, it is 'the Lord who prospers them'. The language they use often savours of cant, and there may be sheer hypocrisy sometimes, but in general their religion is to them a daily reality, and they are content in it and untroubled by doubt. If their souls are shaken it is by the personal sense of sin and of the need for salvation, not by revolt against the weariness of life and the hollowness of religious professions, nor by any doubts as to the foundations upon which the whole structure of organized religion is reared.

Those of this social grade who belong to the Church of England, make less display of religion than their Nonconformist brethren, and except in the extreme Low Church section, are not so prone to invoke the sense of sin. They take religion more easily, but in a very simple, unquestioning, wholesome spirit.

A little lower in the social scale, among those of inferior rank in the same professions, men of business in both wholesale and retail trade, with 'lower division' civil servants and an enormous variety of salaried people, we have a heterogeneous group of whom it is even more difficult to speak as one class.

The oratorical division of our population into 'masses' and 'classes' entirely omits this great section, and yet it is, perhaps, mainly of its members that most large general audiences gathered in any part of London are constituted. The word 'popular' is invariably used to describe these audiences, to bespeak their presence, and to characterize the entertainment offered, as well as the prices which, it is inferred, will be readily paid. Whether for theatre, concert, or exhibition, these people can afford to pay their way, and they form the bulk of most religious assemblages. I have elsewhere spoken of them as the new middle class, and though in strict arithmetical sense somewhat above the middle line, the social position which they hold between the masses and the classes is truly a central one.

But the limits are not well defined. The ranks of this body are constantly recruited from below; and while some may fall back, others pass on, from them or through them, to the ranks above.

It is impossible to estimate with any exactness or certainty the proportion of this large and much mixed section of the people, that may be regarded as religious; but many of the Nonconformist churches are entirely filled from it, as are most of the great preaching mission services, while many scattered members attend the Church of England. They value greatly and therefore seek the social side of religion, but furnish devoted workers and hold their religious opinions firmly. These opinions they have generally inherited and, on the whole, rarely change. Among the great variety of doctrine and practice offered in any neighbourhood in London, the various members of this class can usually find some church or chapel that will suit them.

I have made no attempt to classify those whose rank is the stamp of Education or the seal of Art. On them, whatever their social grade, organized religion has less than average hold. They too, each in their own way, are teachers and preachers.

No class lines in England are strictly maintained; everywhere there is some interchange between class and class, but the uncertainty of the division between lower middle and upper working class is quite special in character, and may perhaps point to a coming change of great importance, if it should indicate a diversity of status amongst the working classes that is likely to break up their solidarity of sentiment. In this direction several causes are now operating.

The great section of the population, which passes by the name of the working classes, lying socially between the lower middle class and the 'poor', remains, as a whole, outside of all the religious bodies, whether organized as churches or as missions; and as those of them who do join any church become almost indistinguishable from the class with which they then mix, the change that has really come about is not so much *of* as *out of* the class to which they have belonged. . . . But meanwhile the bulk of the regular wage-earning class still remain untouched, except that their children attend Sunday school.

As regards religious influence the Roman Catholic poor stand out as an exception. They constitute a class apart, being as a rule devout and willing to contribute something from their earnings towards the support of their schools and the maintenance of their religion; but at the same time they are great beggars, as well as heavy drinkers, and there is no sign that the form which practical Christianity takes in their case helps to make them in these respects either more self-reliant or more self-restrained.

B

CHAPTER TWO

Practices

THERE are many different levels at which contemporary religious activity in Britain can be discussed: identification, membership, participation and personal devotion. There are also many different ways in which such activity may be discussed, and it would be possible and interesting for example to attempt careful statistical estimates such as those of John Highet in relation to Scotland. But the purposes of this chapter do not require such exactitude and it will be adequate simply to indicate broad orders of magnitude.

In any case the actual figures given always require to be set in a demographic context, and their meaning derives more from that context than from their apparent precision. To understand how important the demographic context can be we have only to consider the impact of a population which has increasing proportions of people in the over-forty age ranges. Other things being equal this would raise the percentage of adults attending church, since larger numbers would be living who were free of the ties which prevent attendance in the child-rearing years of marriage.[1] Or, again, we can consider the obvious impact on religious practice of a change in the sex ratio whereby men come to outnumber women. Some attempt will be made to emphasize the relevance of such factors but it will be impossible in the absence of prolonged research to estimate their precise weight and impact. It would take a great deal of time, for example, to document conclusively lower levels of fertility among practising

---

[1] Perhaps the positive effects of an older population are partly counterbalanced by the proportions with infirmities which make attendance difficult.

Anglicans and Free Churchmen than in the population at large. Again, it is very difficult to assess whether the proportion of one male in six working on a Sunday substantially affects attendance or itself reflects indifference.

There are other difficulties which are worth a preliminary warning, but which would be tedious to discuss at length. One is the different criteria of membership employed by the various bodies. Both the Roman Catholic and Anglican Churches for example employ criteria which assume entry by birthright signalized or realized at Baptism. Religious identity is sometimes treated almost as if it were transmitted physically. By contrast the Baptists acquire members only by adult conviction as signalized in ceremonial immersion. Between these two extremes, Methodist and Congregationalists admit to the religious community in a very limited way by infant baptism but only count those who are definitely adult members. A 'real' Methodist is a 'card-carrying' member.[2] Thus in dealing with Free Church numbers, one must reckon with a fringe of 'friends of the congregation' or adherents.

Another difficulty is the varying meaning or importance attached to a similar practice in the two different churches, or for that matter in different branches of the same church. Such variation may seriously vitiate comparisons, and particularly so where Protestants and Catholics are being compared. Obviously attendance at Sunday Mass has much greater salience in the Catholic scheme of values. One feels hesitant about ascribing greater comparative strength to Catholicism simply on the basis of this comparison; and there must be even more hesitation when one recognizes such factors as the impact of minority status on levels of institutional practice, whether the minority be Catholic or Protestant.

However, if all such complications of context and meaning are constantly kept in mind there are points of interest to be found in the figures and percentages. The appropriate point of departure is the religious constituency: all those who when asked their religion by pollster, army corporal or hospital attendant

---

[2] A. E. C. W. Spencer discusses criteria of membership in 'Notes Towards a Statistical Definition of Belonging to the Church', delivered at the International Conference of Religious Sociology, 1962.

reply Catholic, Church of England or whatever it may be. Obviously these constituency figures will differ according to the total geographical area under consideration or the extent to which children and adolescents are included. Most of the studies on which these remarks are based exclude Northern Ireland; all exclude Eire; and in the case of the ABC TV study, *Television and Religion,* the figures refer to the London, Midlands and Northern television regions only.

Those who identify themselves as Church of England make up two-thirds of the English population, or a significantly smaller fraction if Wales and Scotland are included. The Free Church constituency for the whole country stands at round about one person in ten. Roman Catholic identification reaches roughly the same order of magnitude. The Church of Scotland is of course the majority church in Scotland, but taking Britain as a whole it too has a constituency of somewhat under one person in ten. Thus, these four groupings account for the great bulk of denominational identification, leaving only something under one-tenth unaccounted for.

Of this tenth, about half, possibly a little more, account themselves as not having any religious label. A further one per cent of the whole population is Jewish. This leaves 4% to be divided among the sects, Eastern Orthodoxy and non-Christian religions. The Muslims, Hindus and various Orthodox Communions must each number about 200,000: together 1%. The Orthodox are largely Greek (Cypriot) but there are Russian, Serbian and Armenian Churches also. Between 1% and 2% can be attributed to the small sects (Witnesses, Pentecostalists, Christadelphians, Gospel Halls, Brethren of various kinds and so on). This is the kind of maximum figure which emerges if one takes an average based on comparisons of local surveys.

Once one turns from the question of identification, the picture becomes very much more complicated: initially it is simplest to discuss various kinds of membership and participation before proceeding to the further questions relating to church attendance week by week. For these purposes each church (or group of churches) must be dealt with in turn. Scotland also requires separate treatment.

The Church of England has been the subject of the Paul

Report, and it is also served by a Statistical Unit.[3] The Paul
Report refers to various aspects of 'membership'; baptism, confirmation, burials and weddings, electoral rolls, Christmas and
Easter communicants. The Established Church has declined in
each of the aspects mentioned over the past sixty years or more,
especially taking into account the rise in population. Baptisms
stood at 650 per thousand live births in 1902, rose to 717 in 1927
and then dropped (especially from 1935 to 1940) until in 1960
they numbered 554. Confirmations fell from 42·8 per 1,000 in the
12-20 age group in 1911, to 34·2 in 1960. Perhaps one ought to say
in parenthesis that sharp falls in both indices over the past four
years or so (1961-5) are largely statistical illusions which have to
be set against the effects of the declining birth rate during 1947-51
in the case of confirmation and very recent patterns of migration
in the case of baptism.[4]

Marriages have fallen from 698 per thousand in 1899 to 474
in 1962, compared with rises in Roman Catholic and civil ceremonies, which in 1962 stood at 123 and 296 per thousand respectively. The peak for 'other religious ceremonies' for marriage ran
from 1874 to 1924, since when they have shared the Anglican
decline. In 1962 they stood at 102 per thousand. Other declines
are noticeable in Easter day communicants, falling from 98 per
thousand (of people over 15) in 1911 to 69 in 1962, and in electoral
rolls, falling from 152 in 1927 per thousand of the appropriate
section of the population to 81 in 1964.

The net result to date is that some 27 million persons in the
provinces of Canterbury and York are baptized 'Anglicans':
66% of the population in those provinces. Over one-third of
these are confirmed : 24% of the population. But only five out of
every hundred make their Christmas Communion and six their
Easter Communion. Of course, all such figures mask considerable variations : as regards Easter Communion, for example,
dioceses like Hereford, Carlisle, Bath and Wells, Gloucester,
Exeter and Chichester range between eleven and seventeen per

---

[3] L. Paul, *The Deployment and Payment of the Clergy*, Church Information
Office, 1964, and R. Neuss, *Facts and Figures about the Church of England*,
Church Information Office, 1965.
[4] My comments on this are printed in a Symposium on Confirmation, published by SPCK, 1967.

hundred persons obedient to their Easter duties whereas dioceses like London, Birmingham, Sheffield, Southwark, Bradford and Southwell range between three and five per hundred. This contrast is substantially an urban-rural one. Moreover, particular urban areas in places like London and Birmingham would show Easter indices as low as 1% if not occasionally lower.

However, at least part of this decline in proportionate numbers must be set against the effects of migration, whereby largely Anglican populations have tended to leave and largely non-Anglican populations have arrived, especially since 1930 and again since 1950. This leads one to a consideration of the Roman Catholic Church, by far the largest beneficiary of mid-twentieth-century migrations from Ireland and the Continent. One must also remember that these migrations have been into the large cities: the decline of Anglicanism in cities like Liverpool and (more recently) London is not simply the effect of town air.

In 1851 Roman Catholics in England and Wales comprised 4.5-5.5% of the population, nearly half of whom were Irish-born. By 1911 the percentage lay between 6 and 7. According to the Newman Demographic Survey this rose to 10.7 in 1951 and 12.2 in 1961. It is from 1910 that all the indices turn upward and they have continued to do so ever since. The proportion of Catholic marriages rose from 4.1% in 1908 to 5.2% in 1919 to 12.3% in 1962; the baptismal birth ratio was 7.7% in 1911, 9.2% in 1924 and 16.1% in 1963.

Apart from migration three factors have been at work in Catholic expansion: mixed marriages, higher fertility and conversion. The most important single factor is mixed marriages. The fertility differential between Catholics and others has been declining. Conversion statistics are very difficult to interpret: all that can be said is that there was an erratic increase from about 7,700 per year in 1911 to a plateau around 12,000 1920-1935, followed by a steep decline down to 1943, a rapid recovery to 12,300 in 1961 and then another decline. Some estimate of the impact of migration may be made from the fact that between 1931 and 1961 the total of Irish-born at each census increased by 128%. Moreover the resettlement of the Polish Army after the Second World War added over 100,000 to the Catholic population.[5]

Of those who can be regarded as part of the Catholic community in England and Wales, some two million attend Sunday Mass: just over 4 out of 10. Some 6 out of 10 claim to attend Mass 'most Sundays', while 7 to 8 are present for their Easter and Christmas duties. This, of course, contrasts dramatically with Anglican laxity: only about one in 13 Anglicans is present at Sunday service.

The Free Churches present a picture of continuous erosion. Initially they seem to have maintained themselves while the Church of England began to decline, but once their own decline set in it was quite rapid. Moreover the loss of influence is greater than it appears since the category of 'adherents' is believed to have dropped from 40% to 10%. Figures given by Christopher Driver indicate the extent of the loss.[6] From 1910 to 1966 Methodists in Britain declined from 1,168,415 members to just over 700,000. Over the same period Baptists in Britain declined from just under 400,000 to 280,000 and Congregationalists in England and Wales from 456,613 to about 200,000. The smaller bodies like the Unitarians, the Presbyterian Church of England, the Salvation Army and the Society of Friends, have all experienced some element of decline as well: between them they number some quarter of a million members.[7] One must also include the Calvinistic Methodist Church with some 130,000 members, the majority of whom are in Wales.

So far as Methodism is concerned net losses have tended to run at about 3,000 a year, with a sharp increase during 1940-1943 and a respite during 1947-1957. Over the years 1963-1965 losses ran again at the level of the early nineteen-forties, but there is reason to suppose that the drop in birth rate during 1947-51 had the effect of exaggerating the 'true' loss for these years by diminishing the inward flow of young people.[8] At the same time the

---

[5] This information is drawn from A. E. C. W. Spencer, 'The Demography and Sociography of the Catholic Community of England and Wales', *Downside Symposium*, 1965.

[6] C. Driver, 'The Nonconformist Conscience', *New Society*, 27 June 1963.

[7] Preliminary reports of an investigation by the Foy Society document this decline for Unitarianism.

position is more dangerous even than it appears simply because the age structure of Methodism, along with that of all Free Churches, is heavily weighted towards the over forties by comparison with the population at large. In this it evidences the reverse situation to that in the Roman Catholic Church, while the Church of England remains more a reflection of the population as a whole.

All in all Free Church membership for Britain (excluding 400,000 identifying themselves as Presbyterians in Northern Ireland) stands at almost 1¾ millions. This compares with the 10% or more who merely identify themselves as nonconformist; a penumbra of residual nonconformity numbering well over three millions. Of the total Free Church community just under a quarter is to be found in chapel each Sunday, while something under 40% attend at least once a month and under 60% 'now and again'. Indeed less than 30% of those calling themselves Nonconformist are entirely outside their churches' ministrations, compared with 40% of Anglicans and 20% of Roman Catholics. Thus the dramatic falls in membership relative to population may be much less dramatic when one considers the total number occasionally going to church.

It only remains now to assess church identification and membership in Scotland, following the researches of John Highet.[9] Some 60% of the Scots population may be accounted members, compared with some 20% in England and Wales. Of these three-quarters are Protestant, and two-thirds Church of Scotland. The other quarter are Roman Catholic: something over half a million persons. Of this total 'membership' about 900,000 (or 26% of the adult population) are present in church on Sunday, somewhat over one-third of these being Roman Catholic. This is a considerably higher proportion than in England, but the Third Statistical Account of Scotland nevertheless persistently remarks on the fact of declining participation over recent years, particularly in industrial districts. It is worth noting perhaps that the half a million Catholic Irish deposited by migration in Scotland

---

[8] See the reports submitted to the 1966 Methodist Conference by the Church Membership Committee.

[9] J. Highet, *The Churches in Scotland Today*, Jackson, 1950, and *The Scottish Churches*, Skeffington, 1960.

(especially Clydeside) is almost exactly balanced by the Scottish Presbyterians earlier deposited in Northern Ireland.

Apart from the membership or other attachment so far discussed, there is a further source of religious interest in the audiences of radio and television. Research by Robert Silvey at the BBC has revealed the extent (if not the quality) of this and the results parallel in some degree the very high participation by radio shown in the earlier study of Cauter and Downham. From the figures supplied by Silvey and from the study *Television and Religion* it would seem that on any given Sunday about 24% of the adult population see BBC religious programmes and about 18% see ITV religious programmes. In general the proportions listening rise with each age group, especially so with respect to 'Songs of Praise', the most popular single programme. On radio the most popular single programme is the People's Service drawing audiences of nearly 9% of the adult population; 'Chapel in the Valley' preceding it earlier on a Sunday draws more like 7%. Draws is perhaps too strong a word, since radios (like TV sets) are frequently just left on whatever is being broadcast, but it may still be noteworthy that these programmes have working-class audiences of three million in the case of 'Chapel in the Valley', four and a half million in the case of the People's Service.

Ancillary organizations provide further avenues of religious participation or influence, especially for the young. Decline amongst these is important because most evidence and common sense suggests that without *some* youthful socialization into religious norms and practices church-going is not likely at *any* point in the adult life cycle. The ancillary organizations are of many kinds, from Mothers' Unions and Darby and Joan Clubs to Toc H and young wives' groups, but those specifically concerned with the young are youth clubs, uniformed organizations and Sunday Schools. So far as Sunday Schools are concerned, diminishing support is quite clear. Church of England Sunday Schools covered 303 per 1,000 of the population aged 3-14 in 1897 and in 1958 only 149, although it should be remembered that Parish Communions now partly absorb the functions of Sunday Schools. In 1910 nonconformist schools covered some three million scholars in England and Wales and in 1962 only

between 800,000 and 900,000. Of those who 'ever went' to any
Sunday School the percentage had dropped in 1957 from 76
among those over 30 to 61 among those under 30. In that year
one person in two claimed to send children to Sunday School,
but in 1964 only one child in seven attended Sunday School
regularly, and if a church service is included, one child in four.
Still, there remains a great deal of support for the *notion* of
Sunday School attendance, and this is presumably linked to
support for religious education in schools and the teaching of
prayers to children. At least four persons in five seem to feel
that religion should be passed on in these various ways to
children.

Boy Scouts, Girl Guides, Boys' Brigade etc. have all been
under pressure, and in the last chapter of this book an attempt
is made to raise the relevant queries about the future of such
organizations. So far as the Boys' Brigade is concerned it ought
perhaps to be linked more properly with Sunday School, the
temperance movement, even the amateur choral society, all of
which in some measure belong to late nineteenth-century evangelicalism and have shared in the general shrinking of the social
area where evangelical ideas are dominant. Boy Scouts are not
of course specifically church organizations, but they do represent
an element of diffuse stoic Christianity based on notions of leadership and example. The national figures show a fairly static situation over the past decade with Scouts and Cubs continuing to
number some 400,000. About half the troops have some form of
affiliation with a church. Concern has shown itself in the Chief
Scout's 'Advance Party' Report, which among other things
suggests ways in which the public image of scouting may be
made less juvenile.

We now come to assess the overall figures for church attendance and to suggest in this respect the extent of decline in
institutional religion since the opening of the twentieth century.
It may be worth remarking that an expanding Catholic population is likely to mask declines for Protestants in the general
figures for church-going, especially amongst the under-twenty
age group.

If we take the *Television and Religion* study, which is based
on England alone, we find 10% declaring they had attended

church the previous Sunday. Some half of these were Anglicans and the rest divided between Free Church (2·75%) and Roman Catholic (2·25%). These figures strike one as odd, especially in their distribution between the churches, and they require comparison with the figures for the whole United Kingdom (including Northern Ireland) provided by National Opinion Polls for Ronald Goldman.[10] This shows 16·9% having attended a church within the last seven days, and of these some 6·2% were Anglican, 5·4% Roman Catholic, 2·7% nonconformist and 1·6% Presbyterian. Obviously the overall figure can rise when the interval of seven days is used: some people might count the period as covering two Sundays. At any rate other investigations on a national scale have arrived at the overall figure of 15% and further evidence suggests that this should be distributed about 5% each to Roman Catholics and Anglicans, 2·5% to the Free Churches, 1·5% to the Presbyterians, leaving some 1% to others of which ·2% represents synagogue attendance.

A rather different picture emerges if we consider the numbers of those who are to this or that degree church attenders. Thus, if one takes the Goldman figures for church attendances in the course of three months, we have a total of 42·6%, distributed between Anglicans (24·1%) Free Churches (5·3%) Roman Catholic (6·7%) and Presbyterians (4·1%). Taking this kind of period brings into better perspective the strength of the Church of England. The position for the United Kingdom might be summarized from a whole series of polls as follows: 15% are present on a Sunday, 20% every two Sundays, 25% every month, 40% every three months and 45% every year. If such figures are a shade optimistic the exaggeration is unlikely to be serious. Some 35% are never in church; the remaining 20% appear for rites of passage and special occasions. It is rather interesting that there are no large increases for major festivals outside the Church of England; and one may suspect that harvest festivals, carol and war remembrance services often rank as major festivals, in the eyes of laymen.

The general tendency to institutional decline can also be traced from local studies, although it still remains difficult to

[10] R. Goldman, 'Do we Want Our Children Taught about God?', *New Society*, 27 May, 1965.

decide whether the current situation represents a trend from the mid-nineteenth century or a trend from the period of the first world war following the 'religious boom' which Wickham analysed in Sheffield from 1880-1910.[11] One cannot help feeling that the first world war was an important factor.

Attention has often been drawn to the studies which Rowntree undertook of York showing a decline of attendance from 35·5% of the adult population in 1901 to 17·7% in 1935 and 13% in 1947.[12]

Similar evidence can be cited for Liverpool, where censuses were taken every ten years from 1831 to 1912. 70% attended in 1831, 30·5% in 1891 and 21·2% in 1912. A further enquiry undertaken in 1934 suggested that 15 to 20% were then attenders.[13]

Particularly useful work has been done by William Pickering documenting the same processes for the two northern working-class towns of Rawmarsh and Scunthorpe.[14] In general he shows there was a quickening of church life up to the first world war, especially among nonconformists. The Church of England fell out of the race first, yet Free Church decline, once it set in was even more apparent.

Taking the Church of England first, Easter Communicants in 1911 represented 3·1% of the Rawmarsh total population and 3·6% of the Scunthorpe total population. Comparable percentages for the two towns respectively in 1953 were 1·6% and 3·1%. For the Free Churches membership dropped in Rawmarsh from 7·2% of the total population in 1901 to 2·4% in 1951. The smaller bodies and sects have remained static, with some gains to Witnesses and Pentecostals and some losses for the Salvation Army and evangelical missions. One suspects this change of balance among the smaller groups is true outside these specific areas. The Roman Catholic community had risen during the twentieth century until in the two towns Easter duties accounted for about

---

[11] In *Church and People in an Industrial City*.

[12] B. S. Rowntree and B. R. Laver, *English Life and Leisure*, Longmans, 1951. In ch. 13 the authors discuss researches carried out in York by B. S. Rowntree over the period of half a century.

[13] D. Caradog Jones, *Social Survey of Merseyside*, Hodder and Stoughton, 1934, vol. 3, esp. ch. 11.

[14] W. S. F. Pickering, *The Place of Religion in the Social Structure of Two English Industrial Towns*, Ph.D. thesis, London, 1958.

2% of the population. Pickering also carried out his own census (1954/5) showing some 7-8% attendance of adults in Scunthorpe on an average Sunday and 6-7·5% attendance in Rawmarsh. One-third of these attendances were Roman Catholic. However, attendance rose to 11% in Rawmarsh and 15% in Scunthorpe on a feast day, and the Church of England then regained its position as having the largest group of worshippers. All the figures for these working-class towns are below the averages for the country as a whole.

If we turn to the rural areas we have the evidence cited by Williams for Gosforth in Cumberland (a county always known for a low level of religious practice) and by Pons for a village in Hertfordshire.[15]

In Gosforth, Williams showed a situation of indifference stemming from clerical absenteeism which went back some four hundred years. The village is almost exclusively Anglican, the nonconformists being confined to the towns. Without any fall in population the average number at communion on a Sunday fell from 11·4 in 1900 to 7·6 in 1950. The only periods of religious activity were Easter, when some 15% made their Easter communion (an increasing number over the present century), and (in terms of the life cycle) during the period immediately preceding confirmation.

The village in Hertfordshire is much less isolated but seems not to have Gosforth's long tradition of indifference. As in Littlejohn's study of a Cheviot village older people remember a period when the church was full. Evidence relating to 1851 suggests that some 30-40% of the village probably attended morning service. Now some 14·5% on the average attend at all on a Sunday, although on great festivals the numbers include about half the village population. Clearly the tradition of 'occasional conformity' retains greater power in the countryside than in the towns or cities. As in Gosforth, the vast majority of inhabitants are Anglican.

These general points about the erosion of religious practice can now be reasonably combined with some comments on the

[15] W. Williams, *Gosforth: the Sociology of an English Village*, Routledge, 1956, and V. Pons, *The Social Structure of a Hertfordshire Parish*, Ph.D. thesis, London, 1955.

kind of variations which exist nowadays as between different kinds of area. Plainly in the examples given the working-class town is below the national average and the rural district in Hertfordshire above it, while a country and market town like York lies between. However, the studies that have been done enable us to note variations found in a much wider range of social area, from pious Herefordshire to irreligious Dagenham.

The areas where practice is least, particularly as regards the Church of England, are undoubtedly new housing estates[16] and old-established working-class areas in large cities. Here Anglican Sunday practice may vary between 0·5 and 2·5% but there is usually a fair-sized Catholic population in such places which pulls up the overall average. Not only is the Sunday attendance very low but the proportion of those never attending is much higher. Thus in Dagenham some 83% 'never went'.[17] In Bethnal Green only 13% attended in the course of a month, which probably means that three-quarters never go to church at all.[18] In the Metropolitan Borough studied by Mass Observation, 18% attended during a month, but the number of those never darkening the church door was still 60%.[19]

Smaller-sized working-class towns are likely to achieve around 7-8% attendance per week: if they rise higher, as in Billingham (15%) or Bolton (20%), it indicates a substantial Catholic population.[20] Crewe, which is very largely working-class, has around 9-10%, but there is a tradition of paternal and even friendly relations in the town through the railway companies which seems to have caused less social alienation.[21] Market and country towns, even when based on industry, seem to have higher percentages:

[16] Cf. J. M. Mogey, *Family and Neighbourhood*, Oxford University Press, 1956, esp. pp. 145-147. Mogey suggests increased withdrawal from all communal contacts on the housing estate, even from the contacts characteristic of the 'traditional' working-class area.

[17] P. Willmott, *The Evolution of a Community*, Routledge, 1963.

[18] M. Young and P. Willmott, *Family and Kinship in East London*, Penguin Books, 1962.

[19] Mass Observation, *Puzzled People*, Gollancz, 1948.

[20] Cf. P. R. Kaim-Caundle, *Religion in Billingham 1957-1959* published by Billingham Community Association, and T. Harrisson, *Britain Revisited*, Gollancz, 1961 (on Bolton).

[21] J. S. Cowan, *Church and People in a Cheshire Town*, obtainable from Crewe Public Library.

15 in Banbury, 12·5 in Derby, 17·5 in Glossop. Yet High Wy-
combe has only 10%, conceivably because the Catholic population
appears unusually small.[22]

Suburbs also appear to be places of relatively high practice, and
they are the only areas outside traditional market towns or
country districts where Anglicanism recovers some of its dominance. Woodford for example achieves 15% practice, and in the
course of a month 34% of the middle class and 17% of the working class are found in church.[23] It seems that in a socially varied
area working-class practice may not be quite as low as where the
class affiliation is entirely monochrome.

Patterns of observance within England are plainly connected
with complex variables relating to region, class and size of town.
Gorer in his study shows a series of clear connections, even when
the distribution of the Catholic population is allowed for.[24] Thus
cities over a million have lower practice than those over 100,000,
and the number rises again for towns under 10,000. The north
is more practising than the south, and the south-west more
practising than the south-east. The upper middle class is more
practising than the lower middle class, and a large gap yawns
between the lower middle and the working class. Presumably
one aspect of this class differential is the increase in practice with
each rise in educational level.

Of course there are also variations by denomination in terms
of region and class. Regionally Catholics are concentrated in
the north-west and the London area: they are very infrequent
in country districts, and the south-west. Nonconformists are
strong in the north-east and parts of the south-west (especially
Cornwall).[25] The Church of England appears strongest in Norfolk, Lincolnshire, and the West Midlands. Jews are almost en-

[22] Information is taken from M. Stacey, *Tradition and Change: a Study of
Banbury*, Oxford University Press, 1960; T. Cauter and J. S. Downham, *The
Communication of Ideas*, Chatto and Windus, 1954; A. H. Birch, *Small Town
Politics*, Oxford University Press, 1959; and B. R. Lavers and B. S. Rowntree,
English Life and Leisure.

[23] P. Willmott and M. Young, *Family and Class in a London Suburb*,
Routledge, 1960.

[24] G. Gorer, *Exploring English Character*, Cresset Press, 1955.

[25] See the maps of religious distribution provided in the *Reader's Digest
Complete Atlas of the British Isles*, 1965, p. 120.

tirely confined to a few large cities, particularly London. Within London itself of course there are religious concentrations by areas: Jews in a comfortable suburb like Golders Green, Catholics in Stepney, Westminster and Marylebone, where they constitute nearly half the population. With the partial exception of the Baptists, nonconformists are weak in London. Such ecological distributions largely indicate the class variations between the denominations. Catholics are largely concentrated in the working classes, the Free Churches in the lower-middle status groups,[26] (especially teachers, clerks and shopkeepers) while the Church of England reflects the social structure as a whole, except that practising Anglicans are strongly skewed to the more prestigious strata.[27] Free Churchmen are internally differentiated: no one has ever located a proletarian Quaker or (except in Lancashire) a working-class Unitarian. Of the major denominations the Baptists probably have comparatively more in less honorific professions. It may also be the case that persons of no religion are more frequent in professional strata: Birch's evidence for Glossop certainly suggests this,[28] and the phenomenon of explicit irreligion *and* high practice at universities is consistent with it.

The class distribution and social mobility of the various religious groups is usefully illustrated by the kind of information available about two status groups: university students and politicians. Anglicans are relatively more dominant and Catholics more infrequent at Oxford and Cambridge. Given their age structure the Free Churches seem over-represented at universities other than Oxford and Cambridge and Catholics underrepresented. Presumably denominational evaluations of education and reactions to mixed education have some influence here.

One would also like to know if Catholics are especially conspicuous by their absence from science faculties, though this may not be the case since these are more open to less honorific strata,

---

[26] It is a little puzzling to find almost the same proportions of self-identified Free Churchmen in the upper and lower-working-class strata as Roman Catholics. One would like to know the status differences between practising and dormant Free Churchmen, particularly by area. Our ignorance about the Free Churches underlines the call for a 'Paul Report' made at the 1966 Methodist Conference.

[27] As e.g. in A. H. Birch, *Small Town Politics*.

[28] Birch, *op. cit.*

particularly engineering. Jews are probably over-represented in universities, and are especially numerous in the comparatively agnostic, cosmopolitan and socially open University of London.[29]

Evidence on politicians is available in a series of books on British elections and in Guttsmann's *British Political Elite.*

The distribution of religious allegiance among politicians provides an excellent index of the alignment of religious forces in the overall structure of class, status and power. W. L. Guttsmann has documented the historical connection of the Liberal Party with Nonconformity and the traditional ruling class with Anglicanism. Thus politicians coming from the landowning class or educated at the seven *élite* public schools have been overwhelmingly Anglican.

It is significant that no dissenters have ever achieved the prime ministership in a Conservative government, unless one counts Neville Chamberlain. The case of Chamberlain is itself instructive since the family connection was Unitarian and in only the previous generation vigorously radical: otherwise the chancellorship represents the furthest extent of dissenting penetration— for example Kingsley Wood and Selwyn Lloyd. It is generally the case that the non-Anglican background of conservative leaders is a generation or more in the past: Baldwin for example, or more recently Enoch Powell. But in Liberal or Labour governments the prime ministership has been freely available: Campbell-Bannerman was a Presbyterian, Asquith of Congregational background, Lloyd George a Baptist, Harold Wilson is a Congregationalist, while Ramsey MacDonald had connections with the Fellowship of the New Life.

The same pattern has been repeated for all parliamentary candidates at each post-war election as documented by David Butler and his collaborators. The connection between the Conservative candidates and Anglicanism is quite clear, and so is the association of nonconformists, Jews and Roman Catholics with the other parties. The figures given almost certainly minimize the non-Anglican totals but there is no reason to doubt the distribution of political allegiances which they reveal.

The Labour connection is particularly clear with noncon-

[29] Information partly drawn from J. Brothers, 'Religion in the British Universities', *Archives de Sociologie des Religions* 18, July-Dec. 1964.

formists and Jews, less so with Roman Catholics. It also emerges that those non-Anglicans standing as conservatives are on the average only allowed in constituencies where they are less likely to be elected. Thus in 1954 of 82 non-Anglicans standing as conservatives only 23 were elected in a house almost half of whom were conservative, whereas of those 153 standing as socialists, 94 were elected. To some extent these figures exaggerate the socialist commitment of nonconformist politicians, simply because those who stand as Liberals are not adequately recorded and in any case hardly ever elected. Nevertheless two Methodist and two Jewish M.P.s on the Conservative side and twenty-nine Methodist and thirty Jewish M.P.s on the Labour side are a clear enough index of the fundamental situation. The class mobility of the various groups is further indicated by the existence of thirty-two Jewish M.P.s drawn from 1% of the population, fifty-two non-conformist M.P.s based on 12% of the population and only thirty-two Roman Catholic M.P.s, again based on some 12% of the population.

Finally, there are certain general points to be made about institutional practice in Britain. Most important is the striking resilience of the churches under unique pressures, accelerating social changes and the kind of rapid social movement which erodes stable institutions of any kind which do not happen to be part of the required structure of Government. The constant use of the word 'decline' needs to be set against massive exchanges of population by migration which inevitably lowers the proportion of practising Protestants. It may also be that almost the same total number of people come to church but simply appear less frequently: certainly the virtual disappearance of attendance twice on a Sunday affects the size of congregations. At any rate the important and massive fact remains that with every incentive to spend time in an alternative manner one quarter of the population is in church at least once a month. And even if one allows for some tendency to exaggerate attendance on the part of those interrogated, that exaggeration is in itself significant.

Of course, there are crises: but these are often occasioned by a certain confusion of role amongst clergy, even a tinge of the masochism which prefers to believe that the 'worst' is happening rather than accept a fairly stationary position: maybe this has had some impact on the special difficulties of clerical recruitment since 1964. Certainly the masochistic element seemed evident when very recent declines in confirmation and baptisms were treated out of demographic context and hailed as 'signs' of the secular society. Yet if we except some mild erosion of the more conventional rites of passage and the special difficulties of non-conformists, the position seems to have been almost stationary since the war. Let it be said quite simply that in the course of a year nearly one out of every two Britons will have entered a church, not for an event in the life cycle or for a special personal or civic occasion, but for a service within the ordinary pattern of institutional religion.

CHAPTER THREE

Attitudes, Beliefs and Opinions

THE beliefs of Britons can be discussed in general or in terms of certain large scale sub-systems of belief. We begin with a general discussion, and clearly this will also serve as a guide to specifically working-class beliefs since people within that stratum compose at least 70% of the total population.[1] The second half of the chapter will describe the more important sub-systems.

It is worth observing at the very outset that one must beware of simple deductions from figures showing either how many believe in God or how many call themselves Christian. When R. T. McKenzie examined the actual attitudes of those who called themselves 'Labour' he found they cherished many beliefs more consonant with the official beliefs of the Conservative party. The same caution must be observed towards the actual attitudes of those who call themselves 'Christian'. Similarly, the figures which suggest the smallness of the 'orthodox' minority deserve comparable caution. There are many different possible combinations of belief apart from the orthodox which equally have their own internal logic: diversity is not necessarily either confusion or irreligion. To believe in the resurrection of Christ but not *necessarily* in one's own personal immortality is logically possible, although in fact it probably means that some people more easily accept historical assertions than they do metaphysical affirmations.

[1] Most of what follows is based on G. Gorer, *Exploring English Character*; the ABC Television publication *Television and Religion*, University of London Press, 1965; a Gallup Poll Summary of their information on religion, 1957, privately circulated; B. L. Laver and B. S. Rowntree, *English Life and Leisure*; T. Cauter and J. S. Downham, *The Communication of Ideas*; Mass Observation's *Puzzled People*; and R. J. Silvey, *Religious Broadcasts and the Public*, BBC, 1955.

Nevertheless, confusion there certainly is. The splendid study carried out by Mass Observation in a London borough summarized the situation as follows. 'Of the doubters, agnostics and atheists in Metrop., over a quarter say they pray on occasions to the God whose existence they doubt. One in twelve went to church within the past six months, compared with one in three of those who say they believe in God. Over half the non-believers consider there should be religious education in schools.

'Of those who say they believe in a Deity, one in five are definite in their assertion that they do not believe in a life after death; one half say they never go to church, or only go for weddings, funerals, and such-like. A quarter never pray or pray only in church.

'Of those who attend Church of England services regularly or intermittently, one quarter do not believe in an after-life—on the other hand one-fifth of those who don't go to church at all do believe. Of those who don't believe in a Deity or are agnostic nearly a quarter tend to think that Christ was 'something more than a man'; on the other hand, a rather larger proportion of Church of England churchgoers say he was *only* a man. Of those who say he was only a man, one in five also say they believe he was born of a virgin. But of those who attend Church of England services one in four doubt the doctrine of the Virgin Birth, and only one in three give quite definite assent to it.'[2]

Other studies, notably those of Gorer, Zweig, R. J. Silvey, Laver and Rowntree, Associated Television and the Gallup Poll, broadly bear out the conclusions of Mass Observation. It is these which form the basis of the following comments. Precise percentages are mostly omitted, partly because they suggest a bogus precision, but also because anyone interested in the detailed verification or elaboration of these statements should consult the studies themselves. We begin first with dogmatic beliefs. Then moral opinions, attitudes to religious observances, attitudes to religion and to the church are examined in turn. In a general common-sense way it can be assumed that on all points women are more religious than men, the old than the young, the upper than the lower social strata, the north and west more than the south, and that church-

[2] *Puzzled People*, p. 18.

goers are more 'orthodox' than non-churchgoers, particularly churchgoers of the Roman Catholic faith.

If one were to place different beliefs along a scale from the highest degree of assent to the lowest, the highest would begin with belief in God, and run through faith in prayer, acceptance of Jesus Christ as 'Son of God' down to beliefs in hell, the devil and the entire literal truth of the Bible. Nearly nine out of ten believe in God while just over one in ten accept the entire literal truth of the Bible.

But what is meant by belief in God? To some extent the 'High God' of Christian theology seems as remote to Christians as he did to Australian aborigines. But apart from this only some five persons in ten define this 'God' in personal terms and almost the same proportion definitely accept the likelihood of 'life after death'. Neither the 'personal God' nor 'life after death' are usually understood in traditionally orthodox terms but it may be significant that about half the population accept the two beliefs which together could be regarded as the minimum of orthodoxy. Of course it is always possible that the rejection of a 'personal God' sometimes reflects quite orthodox objections to anthropomorphism. Other theists prefer terms like 'life force' or 'spirit', and Zweig has commented that cosmological language about God is more frequent than biblical or theological language. Only one person in twenty is an explicit atheist.

Veneration for Jesus Christ as in some sense uniquely representative of God is found among two persons out of three. This contrasts oddly with the lower level of belief in life after death, and the difference is not easily explicable. Indeed, the extent of agnosticism about the life of the world to come even among churchgoers is a considerable problem, since in this respect Britain is less believing than almost any other nominally Christian nation.[3] A partial explanation may lie in the fact that in Britain Christian doctrines are passed on through the education

---

[3] In *The Deployment and Payment of the Clergy*, Leslie Paul cites a local survey where the incidence of this belief was almost identical among those who were 'churchgoers' and those who were not. This is not borne out by other evidence, but the existence of substantial belief outside and substantial unbelief inside the institutional church on this and other matters is well authenticated. For a general comparison with other countries, cf. *Public Opinion Quarterly*, 1965.

of children in day schools or Sunday schools, where the issue of life to come is not prominent, but this only pushes the problem one stage further back, since disused hymnals remind us just how prominent it once was. The curious and extraordinary variety of conceptions about life after death is well documented by Gorer and includes the astonishing figure of one person in ten who believes in some form of reincarnation. It also seems some 10% of atheists believe in immortality.

Faith in prayer is wide and deep even among agnostics. One person in three says daily prayers (especially women) and only one person in four fails to teach prayers to children. Some 60% have 'some belief in prayer' while only one half of the non-churchgoers are doubtful whether prayer is answered.

About as many believe in hell as believe in ghosts : one person in six. A rather similar number accept the fundamentalist or 'conservative' view of the Bible. Nevertheless only one quarter of the literalist believers feel that their attitude to the Bible is a necessary adjunct of Christianity. At the same time rather few people, at least among churchgoers, feel any reverberations from the classic struggle between science and religion in the nineteenth century over the accuracy of the Bible. The only attitude which may include some echo of old controversies is found amongst that half of the population which regards religion as 'old-fashioned'.

A broad assent exists to what is perversely believed to be 'Christian' morality : do-as-you-would-be-done-by is the most frequently quoted summary of morals. It is as a basis for morality or 'civilization' that Christianity is so widely applauded, and especially as a means for inculcating distinctions between right and wrong amongst children. The sanction of morals usually lies in such popular phrases as 'honesty is the best policy', or 'it's the way to get the best out of life', although churchgoers more frequently than others see this sanction either in an altruistic concern for one's neighbour or in the simple fact of the Church's teaching.

Moral evaluations broadly follow the lines suggested in the fifth to the tenth commandments, with stealing and cruelty regarded as more heinous than lying or adultery. Divorce is a subject where opinions diverge : some two out of 10 would like it to be easier, rather more would like it to be harder, and a third are satisfied with present arrangements. Those who are younger, or male or of higher social status are relatively more inclined to easier divorce.[4]

On other matters of morality there are large majorities opposed to pre-marital or extra-marital intercourse, but especially the latter. Homosexuality is somewhat more tolerated than prostitution, and as regards homosexuality there is an interesting increase in tolerance with the younger age groups. Only one in four wish to punish homosexuality by law whereas two in five wish to punish prostitution. Most people approve of birth control among the married and this includes one-third of practising Roman Catholics.[5]

Attitudes to moral questions not laid down by traditional Christian authorities provide further indications of moral values: drinking before driving, speeding and fare avoidance are widely disapproved, but only about one person in three disapproves of income tax evasion. Only a small minority, even of churchgoers, associate Christianity with teetotalism.

Attitudes to religious observance show considerable variation according to the type of observance. Few consider church-going essential to decent Christian living, not even amongst frequent churchgoers. There is some tendency to associate practice with hypocrisy according to Zweig: this is the most frequent word employed by his respondents. At the same time most people judge churchgoers sincere. Sabbath observance is in evident decline as one moves from those over 30 to those under 30: about 50% of all ages approve professional sport and theatre-opening on Sundays; on the other hand over 50% disapprove of Sunday horse-racing. Only 25% think it wrong to buy objects on Sunday. Sunday Schools attract almost universal approval amongst both those who attend church and those who do not, and in this respect there is little sign of the usual class differential.

Two institutions arousing considerable discussion—the Estab-

[4] R. J. Silvey, *Religious Broadcasts and the Public*, table 31.

[5] *Television and Religion*, table 33. Other tables in this study on which the material in this section are partly based are: 8, 19, 20, 22, 24, 26 and 27. These should be consulted for basic information. Cf. also A. E. C. W. Spencer's paper on this subject published by the Council of Europe Population Conference, 1966.

lished Church and religious education in schools—in fact receive widespread support for their continuance. Religious education may perhaps be considered largely as a means of making social beings out of recalcitrant children, but those who wish to abolish it number only about 1 in 15. It seems that about one person in three would like instruction restricted to scripture only.[6] As regards the Anglican establishment: the form of the coronation, prayers in the House of Commons, prayers in state schools, the provision of chaplains and the general coverage for the whole country provided by Anglican clergy—all receive heavy majority support.[7]

There is, however, an interesting difference between friendliness towards the 'idea of religion' and towards faith, and a certain scepticism (or self-defensive rationalization) about the ecclesiastical institution. At the same time representatives of that institution, the clergy, have a surprisingly good image. In the 'league table' of those who work for the community rather than for self and who exercise beneficial influence they lead doctors, teachers, councillors and Members of Parliament. Clerical unpopularity is very mild compared with that enjoyed by local and central government politicians. Nearly one person in two regards the clergy as underpaid, and recognizes that at least some clergy are seriously overworked. Only one-third of the population has not met its local clergyman, more in London and the Midlands than in the north of England.

A final group of issues concern the churches and social questions or politics. Generally there are more people who would like pronouncements on the former than the latter: two-thirds compared to one half. On social matters the Church is believed to be losing influence and this is widely deplored; its sphere of special competence is defined as illness, death, loneliness, rather than drinking, sexual problems and unemployment. Two-thirds or more consider that the churches are equally concerned for all classes, though the Anglican Church is thought to be a little less equal than the nonconformists and Roman Catholics.[8]

This point is borne out somewhat in terms of the connection

[6] Silvey, *op. cit.*, table 20; R. Goldman, *New Society*, 27 May 1965; *Television and Religion*, table 37; *Puzzled People*, pp. 85-86.
[7] *Television and Religion*, table 19.　　　　　　[8] *Ibid.*

between the Church of England and Conservative voting intention. This connection is strengthened for all denominations when
regular attenders only are considered, but especially so in the
case of the Church of England. One in every two regularly
practising Anglicans votes Conservative and only one in five
votes Labour. Somewhat over one-third practising nonconformists vote Conservative, somewhat under one-third Labour
and one-seventh vote Liberal. Amongst Roman Catholics Labour
voters slightly outnumber Conservatives, and Liberals (7%) are
noticeably less frequent than among either nonconformists or
Anglicans. Thus there is a noticeable skew of practising Christians in the direction of Conservative politics, but it is not without exceptions, nor is it remotely like an automatic assumption.[9]

Five basic sub-systems or patterns of attitudes may be selected
to provide a feeling for the varieties of British religious experience. They are the Catholic, the evangelical, the aristocratic,
the working class and the progressive. It will be noticed that two
of these labels are attached to status groups, whereas the others
are designated as ideological types. This is not to say that these
latter have no specific social locations. Indeed they have. The
'progressives', who have their ideological habitat between the
Observer and the *New Statesman*, are more frequently found
geographically in the triangle formed by London[10] and the two
ancient universities, and in the educated segment of the upper
middle class. The evangelicals are to be found more in small
towns, especially in the regions—Wales, the West of England,
Northern Ireland, Scotland. It is these two groups which are first
of all to be compared and discussed.

It may seem odd to compare the evangelical pattern and the
'progressive' pattern first, but they stand in sharp contrast to
each other as well as somewhat athwart the simple criterion of
respectable affluence which stems from the commercial ethos.
Moreover, the comparison is not merely one of contrasts but of
continuities which are extremely important for understanding
the kinds of religious feeling current in contemporary Britain.

[9] For a study of this whole question cf. R. Stark, 'Class, Radicalism and
Religious Involvement', *American Sociological Review* 29 (5), Oct. 1964.

[10] The relevant districts of London being Hampstead, Highgate and
Blackheath.

Before expounding each in detail it is worth suggesting what these continuities are.

First and above all both types of attitude are very moralistic, the one in relation to the individual, the other with respect to society and politics. The vehicles of this moralism are the pulpit and the literary sermon respectively. The tone is righteous, indeed righteousness is the psychological root from which all else derives. Of course, the 'progressives' acquire an antinomian manner when discussing those individual sins most abhorrent to evangelicals, but in relation to those who lack this antinomian manner they are very righteous indeed.

Second, both traditions value experience. In neither case is this experience treated as a mere means to utilitarian ends in the way business expertise might be. For evangelicals it is essential to have the kind of religious experience which feeds spiritually on the letters of St Paul, notably the Epistle to the Romans. Yet this experience is not graded at all in a hierarchy of approved spiritual conditions: assurance is democratically available. General availability overleaps the bounds of institutional religion and even by extension the bonds of social caste as well: the inter-denominational character of Victorian evangelical religion represented an important break with the practice of social *apartheid*. The rich man in his castle and the poor man at his gate were equals in sin and in the experience of redemption: a point which many rich men in castles found distinctly unpleasing.

By contrast the progressive notion of experience does involve a carefully graded cultural hierarchy, generally based on some concept of an accumulating richness of awareness and intellectual distinction. This richness may be humane in the older sense of a preference for those subjects traditionally thought to foster the finer sensibilities, notably the ancient classics, or else it may be humanistic in that everything is to be understood and empathised, whether outrageously sordid or ridiculously precious. In this latter, more usual version, the concept of Renaissance man, *uomo universale*, indicates a determination to find nothing human alien, except maybe religion. This tradition, whether in its élitist form, chronically afraid of the barbarous masses beating at the gates, or in the form which requires egalitarianism and some identification with the archetypal experiences of the common man sets a primary and profound value on the actual fact of possessing humanity. However, less amiable characteristics include the compulsive need to keep up with the most recent literary fad or artistic gimmick and to ensure that the latest edition of the *Dictionnaire des Idées Reçues* is prominently displayed on one's well-packed shelves. Thus even when progressives do embrace religious practice they do so in the spirit of emulation which supposes that what is good enough for T. S. Eliot, Henry Moore—or even Malcolm Muggeridge—is good enough for them.

Finally, evangelicalism and progressivism value education more than is usual in English society, but whereas for the one education constitutes the basis of an accumulating humane awareness, in the other it is pragmatic and useful. The prime values of progress are assumed to be entirely consonant with education, but in the evangelical case there is always latent tension. The discussion of these latent tensions may legitimately take us into a more detailed separate analysis of the evangelical attitude.

Evangelicals

The evangelical tradition in Britain is an extension of the Puritan spirit as analysed by Weber, but the two are distinct and the later developments in Britain, deriving largely from the Wesleyan revival, received little attention from Weber. Indeed, the following comments may be regarded as a small footnote to his classic work. Particularly is this so with respect to the aspects of Puritanism which Weber regarded as consonant with capitalism and with the development of science: the rejection of magic, personal discipline, thrift, effort, and an emphasis on experience. So far as capitalism is concerned it can be suggested that its late development was less consonant with Puritanism since it involved large-scale gambling. Similarly the development of science made education a danger to Puritanism, partly through an attack on the Bible based on discoveries in geology, biology and anthropology, and partly through the attitude of some psychologists towards the content and dynamics of the Puritan experience itself.

It is worth enlarging a little on the evangelical attitude to education. Obviously literacy is essential to meditation on Scripture and for adequate daily refreshment of the soul. On this point Puritan and Jewish values are identical. Literacy is also essential to achieving or sustaining a decent, probably non-manual job, and security for one's family: particularly was this the case some fifty or more years ago. Thus education served spiritual and secular vocations alike, but it was still not specially valuable in itself, partly for the fundamentalist reasons just cited and also because it could be associated with the indulgent aestheticism of 'high culture': conspicuous leisure, wining, dining, connoisseurship, opera. Evangelicals wished to be literate, not to be literati.

Hence evangelicals persistently attempted to restrict the scope of experience to a context of religious disciplines or at least within such aspects of aesthetic culture as were most easily harmonized with religious aims, for example oratorio. The biblical emphasis assisted here because it allowed a deeply satisfying enjoyment of verbal symbolism while excluding and to some extent explicitly condemning non-verbal symbolism, such as that of art. Thus the word in general became nearly as acceptable as the Word, but the visual symbol was everywhere suspect. This is still the case, although of course evangelicals do not usually see biblical imagery as a form of symbolism but as literally true.

The maintenance of 'experience' within the religious context *sometimes* causes oscillation between personal secular discipline and religious indulgence. It is as if the condemnation of the theatre in the outside world can be compensated by theatricality within the church. The opponents of evangelicalism have often exaggerated the extent of pious emotionalism: the excesses of the American (or Welsh) frontier have been in fact progressively muted until nowadays the campaigns of Billy Graham can hardly be regarded as other than quiet and decorous.[11] The legatees of

---

[11] Billy Graham's campaigns attract large numbers of converts. Very many of these are already churchgoers, and of the minority who are not there is rapid and substantial lapse so far as known church contacts are concerned. At the same time, the remnant that remain to Gideon after the subtractions may be very important; there is some evidence that they become leaders and sometimes enter the professional ministry. Cf. 'The Dr Billy Graham Report' by the Rev. Leslie Harman (Southwark Diocesan Department of Religious Sociology) in *The Bridge*, January 1967, and John Highet's chapter on the 'Tell Scotland' Campaign in *The City of Glasgow*, ed. J. Cunnison and J. B. S. Gilfillan, Collins, 1958 (ch. 22).

the revivalist spasm nowadays are the Pentecostalists. It is also worth remembering that the kind of person who parades with placards in the street is quite untypical of evangelicalism, and that Jehovah's Witnesses and others belong to a quite different and older tradition of Christianity, which is genuinely sectarian in its total rejection of the wider society and in its intense anticipation of an end to the present world order.

Outside their religious practice evangelicals are highly ritualistic in their behaviour. They are restrained and thrifty; they save and buy houses. If hard application and honest reputation brings success in their work it is a 'blessing', though also perhaps a danger. They reject few of the central institutions of society, only certain individual habits, such as gambling and drink, which destroy restraint, encourage fecklessness and exalt chance and speculation at the expense of forethought and work. Hence they achieve a sober accumulation, less of the major capitalist than of the shopkeeper and small business man, or they secure professional advancement by earnest endeavour. With success they are conscious also of the obligations of charity, though they are generally anxious to avoid encouraging the drunken and the idle by easy gratuities. Indeed, they would prefer to give generously to missions and medical work overseas than encourage idleness at home. Above all it is important to be independent oneself and not to rely on the welfare provisions of the State.

These attitudes colour their political views, which emphasize individual independence and are also sceptical of the wholescale moralization of politics, particularly in foreign affairs;[12] in this they present the exact mirror-image of the 'progressives'. They are also well-disposed to alliances with Anglo-Saxon Protestant countries, whereas progressives are (or were) disposed to alliances with Catholic continental ones. Both groups of course are very anti-Catholic, but for the one the European continent is associated with drinking, sexuality and laziness, while for the

[12] For a favourable estimate of the relation of evangelical religion to reform cf. T. L. Smith, *Revivalism and Social Reform*, Harper Torchbooks, 1965. There are interesting comments on a partial breaking of English caste barriers as a consequence of evangelical interdenominationalism as well as on the genesis of the 'good cause' tradition in D. Spring, 'The Clapham Sect', *Victorian Studies* [Indiana University] 5 (1), Sept. 1961.

other it is associated with drinking, opera, and an ulcer-free existence. By the same token the opposition to Catholicism is quite differently based: evangelicals because Catholics are untidy and worship the Virgin Mary, progressives because they oppose artificial methods of birth control and spread superstition.

Amongst certain evangelicals Britain, as she is supposed once to have been, remains the centre of Christian influence in the world. The extreme version of this may be found in the British Israel movement. Milder versions stress Britain's historical debt to Christian values and reformers, and hint that the recent withdrawal of divine support is due to national apostasy and neglect of the Bible. Somewhat secular extensions of both these attitudes —the burden of bearing white civilization and its relation to Christian faith in Britain—may be found along with the gospel of work in a newspaper like the *Daily Express*. But these developments are somewhat at the margin of evangelicalism and are in no way logically or psychologically dependent on it.

There are two further extensions of the evangelical spirit which deserve mention, particularly so since they form an appropriate bridge passage to an exposition of 'progressivism'. The first of these involves a weakening of pietistic pessimism about political action. Just as the older dissent of the seventeenth century acquired tendencies towards a hopeful faith in reason, so evangelicalism, whether Anglican or nonconformist, evolved towards a humanitarian optimism emphasizing the political efficacy of conscience. Initially this might include only rather narrow concerns like gambling and traditional evangelical philanthropy, but it easily broadened out to encompass the liberal peace sentiment and often proceeded further to embrace social reform along a broad front. The autobiography of the Labour M.P. Jack Lawson can give one some insight into the process.

This peace sentiment was not merely the well-known humanitarian concern with war but included a general peaceability and mildness of temperament which really amounted to seeing the world through the spectacles of a nonconformist Sunday School. The older type of Sunday School might have been strongly pietistic, even morbidly so, but the newer type evolved towards an apotheosis of niceness. The crucified Saviour became the

Galilean friend of children. The resurrected Christ was almost lost in the scent of tastefully arranged spring flowers. The grave demeanour of the ancient Puritan dissolved in the smiling parson egregiously shaking hands in the crowded porch.

The ever-smiling witness of humane liberal Christianity introduces the second extension of evangelicalism: spiritual technology, happily more frequent in America than Britain. Classical Puritanism recognized the blessing of God operative in one's secular vocations, but it hardly ventured on the pilgrim way merely as a psychological prerequisite of secular success. It preached peace with God as a consequence of being saved by grace but hardly envisaged a religious appeal based primarily on the psychological and even monetary benefits of a quiet mind. Yet it needed only a change of emphasis and a switching of priorities to produce an approach which justified (say) regular prayer because it prepared one's mind for the rigours of a day in the office. Thus religion became perverted into triumphant living: a constant moral rearmament in the face of modern strains and uncertainties.[13]

Progressives

This spiritual technology, directed towards success, contrasts strongly with the classical Freudian psychology which originally fascinated progressives. But it is not so different from the adapted Freudianism which some 'progressives' utilize to improve their professional performance as distinct from deepening their self-knowledge. However, many of the attitudes and all of the vocabulary differs greatly as between the two systems. Moreover the contemporary fragmentation of sects is if anything greater among the various fashionable psychologies (Kleinian, Jungian, Adlerian, Neo-Freudian, and so on) than among the variants of evangelicalism.

It has been suggested that the supporters of progress are righteous, but this must be qualified. The condemnation may be righteous in tone and intent, but the vocabulary is 'scientific'.

---

[13] Cf. the comments on 'spiritual technology' in R. Hofstadter, *Anti-Intellectualism in American Life*, Jonathan Cape, 1954, ch. 10.

Take for example the following condemnation by Alex Comfort
of Billy Graham's form of evangelicalism: [14]

Sir,

Mr Graham and his converts are of interest in the light of our
need to develop an emotional 'technology', but chiefly as an awful
warning. True, like the psychiatrist, he uses transference to enable
susceptible people to experience and discharge guilt feelings, but he
uses his capacity in this respect to give them an irrational defence
mechanism inaccessible to the intellect.

They feel renewed, their mental states are simplified—oversimpli-
fied in fact—but the experience is not dissimilar to that of a man
who realizes, in a flash of inner light, that all the problems which
have troubled him are due to the machinations of Jews or Jesuits:
the experience conveys a disabling sense of conviction which can
only be challenged at the cost of reviving the old memories.

Mr Graham's converts do not come to terms with such disturbing
matters as their own sexuality or their childhood fears—they paste
a religious ideology over them; if it hardens, they become closed
minds—if it cracks, they are more disturbed than they were before.
The way to deal with infantile anxieties is by experiencing them,
true, but the psychiatrist in facilitating that experience aims to give
adult insight into their basic inappropriateness, not to set them hard
like a plaster image.

A progressive wishing to discredit a particular person or viewpoint does not use the straightforward language of moral dis-
approval but employs the language of pathology. Alternatively
the abusive potentialities of words like paranoia, pathological,
obsessive, etc. can be supplemented by a somewhat imprecise use
of 'Fascist'.

The use of the term Fascist rightly suggests a certain left-wing
commitment associated with a belief in the moralization of
politics, especially issues turning around violence or war. Where
evangelicals often minimize the possibility of large-scale moralization, progressives usually maximize it. Thus they are committed to a whole series of humane causes: the abolition of
capital punishment, freedom from censorship, the right to homo-
sexual behaviour between consenting adults, and—perhaps—
nuclear disarmament. These issues loom even larger than the

---

[14] Letter to *The Guardian*, 10 June 1966.

fundamental reorganization of capitalist society and may even entirely rule out such reorganization. In this way English society has become permeated by causes: either evangelical philanthropy or progressive crusades. The cumulative result has been the creation of a politics of moral protest and a proliferation of pressure groups to ensure this or that reform, from the ending of blood-sports to either the retention or the abolition of the British Sunday.

The key concept for the progressively-minded is freedom, and this achieves peculiar concentration in their concern for the right kind of education. As they are acutely aware of the role of socially segregated education in achieving status, and yet reject the para-military virtues inculcated by traditional public schools and such agencies of secondary socialization as the Boy Scouts, they are in something of a dilemma. They need segregation to achieve a new start in the approved Rousseauesque manner, but they do not want to patronize the cadet corps. To achieve or retain upper-middle-class privileges and to ensure a non-authoritarian environment they need to create specialized schools in which these double aims can be made possible. In such schools children are encouraged to develop sensibility, and sometimes maybe even intellectual values are made the criterion of achievement. Once again a tension develops between the careful psychological manipulation of the permissive environment and the eventual need to inculcate some measure of intellectual or even personal discipline.

Whatever these internal strains, institutional religion is unambiguously identified with the authoritarian and the conventional. To some degree it is possible to sense the correct progressive attitude by inverting attitudes common amongst conventional believers: where an evangelical would be reverential or serious, a progressive should be outrageous or flippant. Prejudice of any kind is greatly disliked unless it be prejudice against members of unprogressive nations or those who can be labelled 'authoritarian personalities'. If people exist who appear to be believers without possessing the authoritarian stigma it is assumed that, like good Jews in other contexts, they are inexplicable exceptions.

Since vocabulary has been mentioned it is worthwhile

emphasizing the role which words play in identifying those who belong to such groupings as the evangelicals and the progressives. Certain words or phrases clearly announce identity or else give right of entry and ensure a preliminary hearing for whatever a person has to say. Among evangelicals, for example, it is necessary to reiterate the phrase 'our Lord Jesus Christ' where a progressive would say 'Jesus of Nazareth' and a Catholic simply 'our Lord'. Again, evangelicals never swear, whereas Catholics use 'bloody' in male company, and progressives use 'God' and 'Christ' as expletives in any company, especially that of Christians.

Thus it is important for dissident persons within a group to reiterate the right phrases even more forcefully when endeavouring to achieve modifications of position, particularly those modifications which move closer to the opposing system. It is also interesting that although many humanists avoid religious vocabulary on account of the structural opposition to institutional belief or even simply on account of cultural embarrassment and snobbery, yet the content or logic of their belief is frequently very similar. Hence it is possible for evangelicals and progressives to hold views which are identical in logical structure but totally opposed in verbal colouring, just as it is possible for the structure of thought to cross the lines of formal demarcation while appearing to be entirely and dogmatically committed to the verbal symbols of exclusive identification. It is this kind of complication which needs to be remembered when considering apparent continuities of thought as well as apparent oppositions, even though continuity and opposition are undoubtedly present.

Stoicism: Elite and Proletarian

If it seems strange to discuss the evangelicals and the 'progressives' together it may seem even stranger to discuss the 'upper classes' and the 'working classes' together. Yet there are many points of contact, and the stereotype of English religion is broadly derived from them. Obviously this is no place to attempt a precise demarcation of their respective social locations: it will have to be enough to indicate that one group may be found in Belgravia and Cheltenham and the other in Rotherham and Scunthorpe. The plural in 'classes' suggests the wide range of attitude and of internal status differentiation within the two groups, and in the case of the working classes at least, considerable regional variation. Parenthetically, it will be understood that I am omitting the Roman Catholic Irish working class in Lancashire, London and elsewhere, simply because it is a separate culture so far as religion is concerned.

On two points the attitudes at the extremes of the social spectrum are identical: in equating religion with conduct and in regarding one's beliefs as inappropriate for general discussion. Religion is equivalent to decency, and in the one case this may include attending church or running one of its organizations, and in the other case not. The universal reticence which goes with this emphasis on decency is partly a fear of ridicule, partly a wish to avoid any hint of contamination by religious fanaticism. The fear of ridicule is related to a masculine ethos which regards religious practice as appropriate for children and women, along perhaps with all the gentler arts. The English male is supposed to live up to an ideal of psychological opacity and cultural philistinism, and it may even be that this ideal is quite frequently attained.

Apart from giving way to unmanly introversion an 'interest' in religion would conflict with a decent indifference to intellectual debates and metaphysical queries. One has one's simple metaphysic but it is not proper to discuss it or subject it to intellectual elaboration. Dogma and theology in religion (as in politics) are symptoms of diseased intellectual enthusiasms which portend the ruin of the state. In a curious way this is one more indication of the close relation between the English political and religious styles: their Laodicean indifference to doctrine and advanced incapacity to understand the logic of discussion.

It may be significant that the upper and working-class styles link a masculine ethos and intellectual indifference with an evaluation of sport which conflicts sharply with that of progressives and to some extent with that of evangelicals. Zweig has described the diversion of religious enthusiasm from the churches to the field of sport. This is a well-worn theme of the English passion for 'le sport', but it remains as true as it is hackneyed, and even clergy feel the need to simulate a passionate concern in the major and minor festivals of the sporting year and its local patronal saints. A clergyman faced with one of those informal occasions where an event for children has induced wives to bring along their husbands will almost invariably refer to the sporting event of which they are being deprived, or pretend that he must close the meeting on time because he is himself desperate to watch the local team on television.

In commenting specifically on working-class attitudes to religion one is embarrassed by richness of materials. The researches of Rowntree and Laver, Zweig, Hoggart, Harrisson, Pickering, and the work of Mass Observation in *Puzzled People* have provided mutually supporting insights with which personal experience largely concurs. Perhaps it should be said that these researches suggest a continuum of approval running from Christianity and religion on the positive side to church and clergy on the negative. Broadly, the universe is accepted as meaningful in a religious sense, and the artisan agnosticism of the late nineteenth century affects only a small minority. To declare oneself an atheist is to run the risk of being accredited with other forms of explicit deviance, as well as defying the taboo against over-precise intellectual standpoints. To be a practising atheist probably indicates political oddity, just as to be a practising Christian is a sure sign of social aspiration or 'hypocrisy'.

'Hypocrisy' is the main epithet applied to those with church affiliation and it is almost universally maintained that those who do not attend church are as good as those who do. 'You don't need to go to church to be a good Christian' is the nearest thing to a fundamental creed amongst working-class people. It may also be suggested that what goes on inside a church is out-of-date mumbo-jumbo. This puzzlement at liturgical complication is very genuine and particularly concerns the Church of England, in which every new ritual quirk or even reform devised by clergy only deepens the conviction that this is not designed for people 'such as us'.[15] It might also be said that if an attempt were made to bring the services up to date and if parsons were to step outside the prescribed role of persons with cultured voices who do not understand the mysteries of the working man's way of life, then resentment would be even greater than it is.

[15] This is documented in T. Harrisson, *Britain Revisited*.

Something further should be said about the role of the clergy in relation to working-class perceptions of it. The cleric is at the same time an object of respect and suspicion, as well as being a figure of derisive affection in the world of the comic cartoon. He presides at the rites of passage, like the churching of women,[16] which are often of very great importance in working-class life, especially those which provide the major gatherings (or even bickerings) of the wider kin. But since this is the only 'visible' portion of his work he is regarded otherwise as a man whose rather easy task is that of entertaining the womenfolk. Add to this the fact that he not only has a white collar but one which is turned round the wrong way, and he becomes defined as a man with 'a cushy number'. Even the industrial chaplain intruding delicately into the factory structure will be asked how he would like to work for a living. This often has an effect on the clergy-man and makes him defensive about the fact that he is resting while others work and *vice versa*. He no longer retains the secure *apatheia* of an eighteenth-century Parson Woodforde but seeks for a role validated by the state (such as social work) and precisely delineated in a way which avoids embarrassment. He is a man with a diffuse role in a situation where that role is culturally restricted merely to the major points in the life cycle.

Apatheia, with other stoic virtues, properly links this discus-sion to the 'religion' of the upper classes. Stoicism is indeed the operative faith of the social *élite*, mingled with a deep sense of what it means to say *Civis Brittanicus sum*. For them, as Words-worth put it, Duty is 'stern daughter of the voice of God'. Further-more, it is God, the Supreme Being, rather than Christ the Saviour who forms the centre of worship: salvation is a word which belongs to the world of indecent enthusiasms and non-conformist fervour. Nothing indeed could be more untoward than an outbreak of religion in the Church of England, which is to be preserved, as one Member of Parliament put it, as the 'main bastion between ourselves and Christianity'.

Duty is the obligation to lead: to run the Mothers' Union, the WVS, the Red Cross, and so on. To lead is to set an example to lesser breeds within the law, and this means that causal connec-

[16] For example in Bethnal Green, according to P. Willmott and M. Young, *Family and Class in a London Suburb.*

tions are believed to exist between *élite* behaviour and public morality in general. To be a prefect brings responsibility. It does not mean obtrusive piety, but it requires the performance of external rituals associated with one's station: maybe the reading of a lesson at Matins, attending a church parade, or else a care for the maintenance of the church's fabric because it is a symbol of national and perhaps familial continuity. Something would be gone from life if the church bells ceased to peal out over the peaceful shires.

So secure and easy are the relationships of these strata with the church and so certain are they that it is their very own institution that it becomes possible for a tradition of dissent to exist among them which arouses mild surprise rather than antagonism. From Frederick Maurice to Archbishop Temple and Canon Collins there can be traced a continuing social criticism by which the traditional care sometimes exercised towards inferiors becomes transmuted into political radicalism. This is even occasionally to be found amongst county families like the Cripps and the Aclands whose sincere meditation on the actual content of Anglican Christianity as distinct from its formal observance has activated continual protest. The difference between those who regard religion as an aspect of status and those who regard it as a personal commitment is summarized in the distinction between 'Church of England' and 'Anglicanism'.

'Catholics'

The Catholic group of attitudes resembles the evangelical only insofar as its institutional form in the High Church wing of Anglicanism is the visible tip of the iceberg. Otherwise there is an obvious contrast with evangelicalism: the emphasis is on institutional tradition rather than the Bible, the visual symbol rather than the verbal; and a comprehensive dogma replaces a stereotyped scheme of psychological dynamics.

All this barely requires rehearsal, but it is worth remarking that, even as an attitude *within* the Church of England, Catholicism is capable of mutations which now render it less militant than once was the case. Partly this is because ritual and visual symbolism can not only form alliances with dogmatic vigour but also dissolve doctrine in poetry, almost indeed in anthropology. Gorgeous rites may even fill the empty spaces which remain when doctrinal rectitude has felt the corrosion of liberalism. Hence the liturgical impulse is released from its channel of dogma and influences institutions like the Family Communion and movements like Parish and People which nowadays include a kind of modernist very different from the old-fashioned variety associated with Bishop Barnes and Canon Major.

There is an additional source of difficulty for Anglo-Catholicism proper. One of its original impulses lay in the restoration of clerical authority and perhaps by implication social authority in general. The Roman Church was used as a yardstick of authority and also of certainty in a world given over to accelerated change. Hence the concern for ritual rectitude and an over-conformity to Roman practices which was often more Papist than the Pope. But *aggiornamento* in contemporary Rome makes all this much more difficult to sustain, and Anglo-Catholics are left isolated, frozen in postures reminiscent of Pio Nono. They thus have no more imposing point of reference than the kind of Roman Catholic conservative (often a convert) who characteristically comes to the surface—in England at least—in a movement like the 'Latin Mass Society'.

A cleric like Hawker of Morwenstowe may stand as a representative of the older Catholicism: sartorially correct even down to the biretta and the kind of rimless glasses favoured by cardinals; representative also in combining the priestly turbulence which terrorizes bishops with an unblinking assertion of ecclesiastical authority. Yet Hawker is now remembered as an archetype of Catholic attitudes much more genuinely popular: the poetry of Christmas and the near-pantheism expressed in the revival of harvest festival. In this way the liturgical rhythms of Christmas and Easter and the seasonal rhythms of rogationtide and harvest can be contrasted with the rude mechanical music of industrialism.

So Catholicism is plausibly linked to all the idealization of Merrie England, the nostalgia for community, the reverence for timbered houses, the extraordinary vitality of the Gothic, and so on through endless derivatives which include the Folk Dance and Song Society, the Youth Hostel Movement, even the Society for the Preservation of Rural England. Indeed since the rural is both more natural and more religious than the urban then it follows that pure food is better than synthetic. Here at least Catholic and progressive can meet on common ground, concelebrating the joys of innocent peasanthood and enjoying the undiluted fruits of nature: St Francis and Rousseau come together at last.

Catholics and Progressives also agree in opposition to the egoism of capitalist civilization. Both admire an organic community in which the unalienated craftsman bends lovingly over his work rather than obeying the monotonous imperatives of the assembly line. After all was not the mediaeval village a commune and the guild a trade union? Capitalism had created a nation of guilt-ridden robots, who either needed a confessional, or progressive education, or both. The answer must be spirituality: mystics of the world unite against the evils of the materialistic West. Only the great spiritual masters of Catholicism and Buddhism understand that superior silence which gives final contentment in a world of hollow men propped up by their own strivings.

At any rate, what began as a movement to bring God back into the Church and to restore the concept of universal Christendom could end by finding him in an English garden. The Church, the garden and the countryside are far from incompatible: after all Vaughan Williams wrote a liturgical Mass as well as Norfolk Rhapsodies and Benjamin Britten sets divine poems by Donne as well as nature lyrics by Hardy.[17] In the end it comes to this—as Bridges so properly expressed it: 'Blessed be the towers that crown England so fair.' The legend of Joseph of Arimathea and the Holy Thorn at Glastonbury is profoundly right: those feet *did* walk on England's mountains green. How should the Almighty and Everlasting God fail to visit his very own people?

---

[17] For a perfect individual exemplification of this group of attitudes I can hardly do better than refer to Frank Howes' comments on Gustav Holst in *The English Musical Renaissance*, Secker and Warburg, 1966, p. 243, in which he sets together a 'mixture of the East, the English folk, and the mediaeval', to which has to be added 'the William Morris brand of Socialism of his young manhood in Hammersmith and the High Church brand of Socialism of Thaxted when he went to live there in 1914'.

Superstitions and Subterranean Theologies

Beyond the kinds of group commitment and class attitudes just discussed there are more diffuse congeries of opinion and belief which are as yet scarcely investigated. These might conveniently be labelled subterranean theologies and superstitions. It may be that subterranean theologies are most frequent in more prestigious strata while superstitions are most common in the working classes.

By subterranean theology is meant a series of interlocking attitudes involving (say) choice of superhuman culture heroes, mechanisms for restoring disturbed moral balances, notions of social cause and effect, diagnoses of contemporary social difficulties, national totems and taboos, and so on.

Only one or two examples can be given. A relatively frequent type concerns precisely the kind of impact of *élite* morals on lesser breed behaviour mentioned above. Thus a letter in a church newspaper declared that the breaking of Princess Margaret's engagement to a man who had been divorced might 'inaugurate a new era in marital relations'. A somewhat different but equally curious notion of social causation is found in the conviction of one Tory intellectual that the Profumo affair was encouraged by the theology recommended in the works of the Bishop of Woolwich.

Another basic type, which involves fundamental symbolism rather than notions of social causation, concerns surrogates for or extensions of the Christian Passion. A particularly striking example might be provided by a television commentary on the Christian Eucharist at the time of Churchill's death which plainly conceived the ceremony as celebrating *his* saving life and passion. Similarly, the sacrifices of servicemen in two wars, but particularly the war of 1914-1918, are regarded as providing a collective salvation through suffering to which the rest of the nation must respond by renewed patriotism and dedication.

Another basic type of belief, again quite different in metaphysical category and in logical structure is a pervasive individualism which takes protean form in economics, politics, art and religion. The individualistic assumptions of independent radical politics as described by Samuel Beer and rooted in late nineteenth-century conditions are paralleled by assumptions about the unlimited economic possibilities open to all individuals who will make the requisite effort. The analogous belief in the sphere of religion rests on the essentially private character of belief and on individual salvation.

The obverse of this individualism is a fear of institutions: either because they are regarded as large, impersonal and sinister, or because one is reluctant to face the structural character of social life and of patterns of commitment. In one sphere this shows itself as a fear of *all* formal leaders, whether they operate in parties, unions or churches. Thus whenever one encounters large-scale objections to the churches one needs to remember that the church is condemned along with *all* mass organization and shares obloquy with the state, the bureaucracy, the unions and the parties. It is institutions as such which are the object of public execration and the adjective 'religious' or 'political' is entirely incidental. The point is quite crucial when one asks the question how it is that Protestant countries can have such high levels of somewhat amorphous belief and such comparatively low levels of institutional practice.

The prevalence of superstition has been documented most usefully by Gorer and it seems that in this connection the usual differentials of belief do not hold or are less in evidence: the male, the young and the working class are not notably less superstitious than others and are sometimes more so. In the matter of ghosts for example scepticism *increases* with age. As it is one in six of the population believes in ghosts and one in fifteen have actually 'seen' one.

Faith in the power of luck and in the usefulness of devices for controlling it in one's own favour is very widespread. One in three of those in the wartime services carried some form of tangible protective magic on their persons. Nearly half the population has consulted a fortune teller, and four out of five read weekly horoscopes, though half of these describe it as 'a diversion'. Yet nearly two men and over three women out of ten sometimes follow astrological advice. No investigation of the precise extent to which spiritualist beliefs are held has been attempted, but there is reason to think that this number, and even the number of those who attend occasional seances, far exceeds the mere 25,000 to 30,000 in actual membership of the two main bodies.

It would seem that vast numbers of people work on the assumption of two basic principles: one is the rule of fate or chance, conceived as rooted in a kind of symmetry (such as that disasters occur in threes), and the other is a 'moral balance', rooted in a universal homeostasis whereby wicked deeds eventually catch up with those who perpetrate them. Certainly people frequently meet disaster with the query 'What have I done to deserve this?', which plainly assumes a moral basis to causation.

These beliefs not only encompass large-scale events but are intimately bound up with the social sanctions which control the intimacies of life and keep one day by day on the right side of the 'powers'. For example, the author once stayed with a student of psychology who became very alarmed when his guest thoughtlessly lifted the teapot to pour out his host's tea. The student then explained that this superstition was one of his many devices for ensuring that he had a 'good day' at the university. At the same time it is known that the taboo on a guest lifting the teapot is related to a need for proper role assignment, originally as between mother-in-law and wife in the latter's house. Now, however, the taboo maintains itself largely as an irrational technique for averting general unpleasantness.[18]

All such examples bear strongly on assumptions about secularization, the impact of the age of science, the advent of human maturity and so on. They suggest that far from being secular our culture wobbles between a partially absorbed Christianity, biased towards comfort and the need for confidence, and beliefs in fate, luck and moral governance incongruously joined together. If we add to these layers of folk religiosity the attraction of Freudianism and of Marxist mechanics for segments of the intelligentsia, it is clear that whatever the difficulties of institutional religion they have little connection with any atrophy of the capacity for belief.

[18] I owe this suggestion to Mrs Mary Douglas.

CHAPTER FOUR

Structures and Patterns

The Wider Context: Theoretical Perspective

THE problem posed at this juncture is the most crucial for our whole discussion: it is the relationship between different ecclesiastical structures and various patterns of society and community in Britain, especially England and Wales.

To understand this relationship properly it needs to be set within the context of wider comparisons. Ideally such comparisons would on the one hand include all cultures subject to large-scale industrialization and on the other hand all cultures which have experienced widespread penetration by the types of religious structure deriving from Christianity. As it happens, these two groups would overlap very considerably but it would be an enormous task to cover all the varied cases, and happily it is not necessary even to try. Some of the major points can be made simply by setting Britain in a comparative context provided by the United States and France. This context is adequate, partly because Britain stands midway between the other two, and partly because France can represent a whole class of Latin countries.

The comparison needs to be made on two broad fronts. The first comprises the shape of social development in the three countries and the sheer historical contingencies on which that shape partly depends. So far as social development is concerned the crucial area of interest turns around the growth or inhibition of institutional means for the channelling of tensions. It may be for example that in one case the inhibition of such institutions builds up to an explosive restructuring of the whole system in which potential antagonisms are progressively polarized, or that in another case the proliferation of varied and accepted dissident institutions builds up cross-cutting identifications at the level of class and nation which allow minor tensions to co-exist with wider unities.

So far as historical contingencies are concerned, these are obviously only partly contingent, but at key moments an event occurs which either permits a particular version of social development or makes it progressively less and less likely. One such contingency is the simple fact of Christianity itself making available certain organizational forms and perspectives (to be described below) which structure the unities and tensions as they occur in particular ways. But at a more local level, there are events like the outcome of the Civil War in England, or the failure of Protestantism in France, or the availability of both Protestant and Enlightenment models of thinking and organization at the birth of the American nation. These are not necessary forms of development but crucial historical junctures turning the 'normal' progress of development in this or that direction.

The second broad front on which comparisons must be made concerns precisely the kinds of religious organization and of modes of thinking made available, in either pure or transmuted form, by the mere massive presence of Christian germination in a pattern of social life over a long period. These germs of thought and institutional form are activated by social development and historical contingency. In turn they colour that development in quite specific ways (even when it strains against the matrix from which it is generated) and control the free play of contingency within a given range of possible options.

Sociologists have developed a shorthand for reducing the infinite variety of these options to three basic 'types' which between them include an enormous range of possibilities. The three 'models', labelled 'church', 'denomination' and 'sect', include most of the basic varieties of organization, religious or political, and many of the basic perspectives, religious or so-called secular, still influential amongst contemporary men. It will be useful to rehearse this shorthand so far as types of organization are concerned before turning to the further question, which is the specific *combinations* which come to exist in a given culture *between* these types of organization, both at the specifically religious level and also so far as political and other organizations take up this or that option amongst the alternative institutional formats provided.

'SOCIOLOGICAL SHORTHAND'*

Church	Denomination	Sect
Claim to social inclusiveness in a given territorial area: either in relation to a given ethnic group (C of E) or universally (RC). Birthright membership.	Hardly ever a social majority; recruited by a combination of original adult self-selection (conversion) or familial tradition.	Usually a small exclusive dispossessed minority; recruited by a combination of self-selection and familial tradition.
Identification with the state or at least general acceptance of political exigencies.	Explicit separation from the state but no rejection of the wider society *per se*.	Radical rejection of the wider society and its institutions.
Examples: acceptance of secular wars, with rather formalistic qualifications in terms of just war concepts.	Acceptance of wars in principle but a stress on the rights of the individual conscience *vis-à-vis* state decisions.	Rejection of secular wars: perhaps a preference for Armageddon.
Sacred hierarchy.	Some pragmatic division of authority roles; some degree of democratic participation, localized in the case of congregational-type religion.	Tendency to reject functionaries.
An objectively valid, essential sacramental system.	Tendencies to subjectivity and personal option in relation to sacraments.	Frequent rejection of sacraments.
Comprehensive dogmatic scheme, often rigid *de jure* and flexible *de facto*.	Emphasis on system of psychological dynamics (conversion process, pilgrim way).	Comprehensive indoctrination.
Crucial dogmatic events in the *past*: perhaps an emphasis on Incarnation and Holy Family.	Crucial psychological event: the repeated *present* conversion of sinners in response to Christ's saving death.	Emphasis on Second Advent in the *future*.

---

* The relevance of these formulations for non-Christian religious is too complicated for discussion here. It will also be recognized that they represent gross simplifications, and are intended as heuristic tools, not substantive descriptions.

Church	Denomination	Sect
Two types: Established churches and diaspora or missionary churches.	*Two types:* Pietist and liberalized.	*Two types:* Perfectionist and antinomian.
Diaspora churches are usually ethnic churches deprived of an exclusive territory (e.g. Irish and Polish RCs in the USA). Like missionary churches they have to accept some degree of pluralism and formal separation from the state. Non-Establishment does not alter their character in most respects: e.g. a hierarchical organicism and an acceptance of political exigency without much criticism *unless* it involves persecution or the promotion of a rival ethnic group.	Pietist type tends to be pessimistic in relation to politics, and, is sometimes inclined to doctrines of Election. Liberalized type includes an optimism either of reason (e.g. Unitarianism) or of sentiment and feeling (e.g. later Methodism).	The two types often involve a polarization at extremes, e.g. complete anarchic individualism (e.g. Ranters) or communism of property and even in sexual relations. There may also be a contrast between the total destruction of the world by an utterly transcendent God and a total immanence whereby 'God' is immersed in the sect members (e.g. Doukhobors).

The Christian 'options' involve systems expressing hierarchy or equality, local autonomy or national and international centralism, bureaucracy or the small intimate group, collusion with the state or rejection of it or co-existence with it, a basis of territoriality or of mutual personal consent, birthright membership or personal choice, etc. 'Church', 'denomination' and 'sect' represent various combinations of these alternatives: for example 'church' represents collusion with the state, centralism, hierarchy, territorially and birthright membership and so on. Taking the simple factor of relation to the state (which will be central to the argument below) the 'denomination' represents friendly but separate co-existence with the state, and the 'sect' total rejection of the state, both of them contrasting sharply with church-state collusion.

Clearly, some of the alternatives mentioned are simply the possibilities inherent in organization as such, but the factor of Christianity makes certain possibilities relatively more available in principle and ensures the existence of specific elements colouring them which are of the highest importance. For example, each of the three combinations of organizational principles is infused with a concept of *the* crucial event. For the 'church' the crucial event (the Incarnation) occurred in the past and has simply to be worked out; for the 'sect' the crucial event (the Second Advent) is to occur in the immediate future; for the 'denomination' the crucial event (salvation by the death of Christ) occurs in each individual soul at some point towards maturity. It will be noted that only in one of these is the 'crucial event' individual, and thus the extent to which the denomination is influential in a given culture expresses, ameliorates and determines a pervasive individualism, which in the case of Britain and America takes varied forms of absolutely central importance: a general distrust of institutions, a preference for psychological over structural explanations, the possibility of an optimism based on individual initiative and mobility, the value placed on conscience, a rejection of holistic or total solutions, a dislike of collective abstractions, and so on.

This is obviously the point at which the combinations of these various structures, the process of social development (industrialization, nationalism, class, etc.) and the crucial historical contingencies, can be brought together with respect to the three cultures to be compared: the USA, Britain and France. Beginning with the historical contingencies it has been suggested that these might be: the dual availability in America of democratic Protestant and Enlightenment models, the outcome of the English Civil War, and in France the failure of the Reformation. Let us take each culture in turn in terms of what followed from these crucial events, selecting two areas of discussion: the extent of polarization of forces in relation to the opposition of classes and to the forces of change, and the accommodation of ethnic minority groups within the overall patterns. We begin with the polarization of forces.

In France the Reformation was crushed and the Roman Church associated with an increasing exercise of central royal authority which allowed little scope for social change. There were no pluralist or working democratic models available and alternative structures had to be elaborated, sometimes in a rather abstract way, by individual thinkers who were progressively more and more alienated not merely from a particular church, but often from religion as such. Thus forces built up within the system which exploded more and more violently as soon as authority initiated the process of change.

The question of religion was posed in terms of all or nothing and the political system developed in a way which placed the forces of tradition and change in dramatic opposition, with the church largely aligned with tradition. Intermediate movements like 'Social Catholicism', 'Solidarism', or even Social Protestantism had no genuine chance: much more likely were the kinds of alignment produced by the Dreyfus affair.[1] Eventually these high tensions were fed into the channel of the Communist party, a political sect proclaiming its own version of total imminent change in the secular order. Thus France became a nation with a higher degree of atheism than any other not under Communist control. Obviously this broad picture of the church opposed by a large political sect is relevant to countries like Italy and Spain.

Turning to America we find that this type of political sectarianism is almost absent. Taking the same kind of historical perspective as that employed for France it is arguable that at the crucial moments of American history the enlightenment concept of a secular state was joined to the availability and familiarity of democratic types of church government on the dissenting (or 'denominational') pattern. Initially some of these had exercised little tolerance towards each other but the inherent pluralism of the varied colonial situation ensured mutual accommodation, aided by the fact that no one group was in a politically dominant position.

America thus had no territorial, dominant inclusive church; only a series of competing religious organization, many of them in any case dedicated to self-government and local autonomy. Moreover, these were increasingly supplemented by religious sects like the Mennonites, Shakers and Mormons some of which could both siphon off some of the extreme tensions and suggest

---

[1] R. Aron has underlined the post-war significance of forces such as those of a 'left' Catholicism, crossing this crucial divide. I follow Aron in selecting the failure of the French Reformation as *the* point of departure for subsequent French history.

dynamic perspectives.[2] At any rate it was not possible for a single organization to so link itself to political authority and the process of secular education that it could become identified with the exercise of repressive or ideological power. Moreover, the circumstances of successive migrations, from the Puritans to the Jews, moulded the concept of America in terms of religious freedom from state interference while allowing America the peculiar glory of being 'one nation under God'. Thus religion became associated with an idealized America and faith could not appear to be compromised by politics.[3] Social change could occur *within* religious groups without any party moving into a stance of opposition to religion as such.

The two cases just described are extremes and indicate how the processes of class, social differentiation and so on associated with early capitalism and then later with industrial civilization can take totally different paths with respect to religious institutions. In the one case all the available models and all the historical contingencies have assisted the survival of uncontroversial institutional religion; in the other they have worked towards maximum tension and massive alienation. The parallel contrast between diffuse faith on the one hand and depth and dogmatic coherence on the other derives from the same constellation of forces.

Britain, more particularly England, can now be set in the same kind of analytic frame; in some respects resembling France, in other (and more fundamental) respects resembling America.

In a formal sense England parallels France by virtue of a central religious body claiming to be inclusive and largely coextensive with the social *élite*. At the same time the association of this church with a centralizing royal absolutism was decisively broken at the Civil War and thereafter the royal power was in any case steadily diminished. This meant that forces did not build up into an explosion in which the church was vitally involved. Instead the tradition of alternative religious bodies and of recognized religious dissent broadened out into an overall

[2] For sociological accounts of these see E. D. Andrews, *The People called Shakers*, Dover Publications, 1963, and T. O'Dea, *The Mormons*, University of Chicago Press, 1958.

[3] Substantially my argument follows De Tocqueville's *Democracy in America*, abridged ed., Oxford University Press, 1946, ch. 19.

pattern of establishment and constitutional opposition both of which usually recognized common religious loyalties beyond their political differences. Even when the disestablishment of the Church became an issue this reflected the vitality rather than the weakness of religious identification.

However, it still needs to be explained how institutional practice in England became suspect whereas the idea of religion or faith did not. To elucidate this fully would require a complicated historical argument.

So far as the Anglican Church was concerned it became culturally separate by virtue of the chasm of class: to be a practising Anglican one was usually either middle class or deferential towards one's betters. So far as nonconformity is concerned the crux turns on its association with Liberalism and the Liberal Party and the problem raised by the emergence of some measure of ideological politics with the growth of the Labour Party. This happened in the following way.

Nonconformity during its period of association with the Liberal Party acquired and propagated individualistic conceptions of social progress, partly by reason of its capacity for individual upward mobility and partly through theological affinity —an emphasis on personal salvation. This placed it to some extent athwart the emergence of the Labour Party, which came to talk officially in terms of structural alterations, and of class rather than individual progress. Nevertheless nonconformity contributed enough to the Labour Party, in terms of models of democratic organization, of personnel and of a pragmatic temper to ensure that the symbols and rhetoric of class struggle were allied to and controlled by a profound individualism. This individualism was shared by nonconformity with English culture at large and continually ensured that political issues were posed even by the 'Left' in the form of moral appeals as well as structural oppositions.

This general individualism became linked to a process of self-identification among working-class people whereby they regarded the personnel of religious bodies either as firmly *élite* or middle class in the Anglican case, or as involved in upward social mobility through educational aspiration or business capacity in the case of nonconformity. In other words, a combination of a suspicion towards all institutions widespread at all levels and of working-class withdrawal from unfamiliar social atmospheres sharply restricted the extent of regular religious practice.

It is now possible to turn, more briefly, to the related questions posed for our three examples by religious development in relation to ethnic underdogs. Obviously this is also connected with the dynamics of class formation since national 'inferiority' may also be class inferiority. In France the obvious case of ethnic differentiation expressed in religious terms is Britanny, but clearly no break is involved with the organic unity of the Roman Church. In America the various migrant ethnic groups discovered in their churches residual foci of cultural identity which in the case of the Catholic groups was further linked to inferior status. Thus religious institutions were at one level vehicles of cultural survival, and at another level either symbols of a long American inheritance (for Protestants) or associated with a group aspiration to enter into that inheritance (for Catholics).

In the British Isles religious dissidence (Catholic or nonconforming), often served to partly express local or national awareness against English dominance. This was in turn then linked to the struggle against English landlords by Irish peasants and Welsh tenants. The Scottish case is more complex, but there is no doubt that the Church of Scotland has been the central focus of Scots' nationhood. Even quite local patriotism, such as that of Celtic Cornwall, achieved some degree of religious differentiation through the spread of Methodism.

Thus the controversial character of religion in France can be related to ethnic and religious unity, while in America and Britain its uncontroversial character can be related to ethnic and religious pluralism. It is now appropriate to turn more directly to the consideration of the form which this pluralism takes in England and then in Wales. So far as England is concerned attention needs to be directed firstly to general patterns of culture and then to the alignment of forces as illustrated in the local situation.

England: Three Cultures – Carol, Hymn and Chorus

Just as English politics run partially athwart official denominational boundaries, so also do patterns of culture. It is not so easy to choose the appropriate symbols for the identification of these patterns, but one of the most helpful is provided by a division into those who sing carols, those who sing hymns and those who sing choruses. The singers of hymns and carols also have special predilections for more complicated music: hymns are aligned (still) with Handel and Mendelssohn, carols with Bach, Byrd and Britten. Needless to say, hymn, carol and chorus can be located to some extent at different intellectual and status levels, the chorus often being a source of social and intellectual embarrassment.

In order to enjoy the chorus one has to be a willing heir to the revivalism which runs from Sankey and Moody through Gipsy Smith to Billy Graham. Among the Free Churches this revivalism finds rather more supporters amongst Baptists than Methodists since the latter have usually succumbed to a tamer style, or even seek again their roots in sacramental practices. Amongst Anglicans the spearhead of 'conservative' Protestantism, not always quite happy with what Huxley once described as the corybantic element, is centred in a fashionable church like All Souls, Langham Place, and joins hands across denominational frontiers at the evangelical conference centre in Keswick. A characteristic lay sponsor of Anglican evangelicalism tends to be a business man or the occasional major-general; both probably as conservative in politics as in theology.

The chorus today is a mutation of a tradition going back to the eighteenth century—back to the kind of rather ornamental dance tune or street song (Helmsley for example) which often accompanied the vigorous theology of Wesley's hymns. The mid-nineteenth-century version usually combined tunes with dotted semi-dance rhythms reminiscent of the music hall, with words strongly characterized by fortitude in life's manifold misfortunes: 'Will your anchor hold in the storms of life?' and 'Hold the fort for I am coming.' Later varieties developed a rather childish vein in choruses like 'I am H.A.P.P.Y.' and 'A little talk with Jesus makes it right, all right.' Nowadays the chorus is improved by arrangement and by rhythmic surprises and harmonization in the Hollywood *religioso* style. Alongside the chorus tradition runs a parallel development of 'sacred song' which more usually exploits the lugubrious aspects of evangelical devotion, for example the theme of the wanderer far from home.

Needless to say neither sacred songs or choruses are too popular at the upper levels of denominational leadership: Moody and Sankey lasted longer on the village harmonium than on the urban chapel organ. Indeed the corybantic aspect of evangelicalism is largely excluded from what is now called mainstream religion. This mainstream has rested since the Victorian period on the widespread popularity of the hymn. It is difficult to characterize the hymn-singing tradition in a few sentences: the major influences at source are Wesley, with his enthusiastic celebration of salvation, and Watts, with his sober appraisal of a cosmic nature completed and crowned by divine grace. Everybody knows that the Victorian period developed a mawkish strain, but such hymns as 'Forever with the Lord' and 'Nearer my God to thee' are not much sung nowadays. Indeed, congregations today are not quite certain in what spirit to sing even missionary hymns like 'From Greenland's icy mountains' with such lines as 'Can we to men benighted the lamp of Life deny?' Perhaps a major shift of taste has been that signalized in *Songs of Praise*, where the world of nature returns, not in the Newtonian phrases of Watts, but in a softer more romantic vein of feeling as with (say) 'Morning has broken like the first morning.'

The alignment of hymns with Handel, Mendelssohn, and what used to be the cantata market, is worth some further reference since popular Protestant choralism once held enormous sway in England and Wales, even to the point of nearly swamping the *élite* tradition of liturgical music maintained in the college chapels and cathedrals. Doubtless this choralism appealed to a somewhat different segment of evangelical sentiment from the supporters of the chorus, even though the two overlapped. Something of the shift which has occurred even within the world of the choral society may be gauged from the virtual eclipse of the Bible-based *Elijah* by the *Dream of Gerontius*, composed by Elgar to somewhat indifferent 'Oratory verse' by Cardinal Newman. Even *Messiah* has become less central and up to quite recently the reputation of Handel himself suffered from a reaction against the mammoth splendours of Albert Hall and Crystal Palace. It has only recovered because the professional middle class has discovered the operas as well as oratorios on such refreshingly pagan themes as *Semele* and *Hercules*. The young, educated, mobile professional does not know his *Messiah* by heart and knows *Elijah* barely at all: such things can be left to choirs of clerks and teachers, miners and artisans in Wales, Yorkshire and the Five Towns. By the same token young professionals have barely any contact with the tradition of hymn-singing: if they do it is through the chorales in the Passions of J. S. Bach, not *Hymns Ancient and Modern*. After all the Bach revival had no embarrassing Victorian associations and might even be linked with the fashionable discovery of jazz. Strange that a *milieu* rejecting the aristocratic Italianate lyricism of Handel because of its lower-middle-class and religious associations should turn to the profound bourgeois piety of J. S. Bach!

Yet in spite of all this there is no doubt that the hymn provides the most resonant evocation of religious feeling in Britain: for more so than the liturgy. The Bible itself hardly rivals it even among the most biblicist of believers. The hymn is the most central item in the religion of Britain, and the singing of 'Abide with me' at the Cup Final or 'Jerusalem' at the last night of the Promenade Concerts remains a witness to its unique place in popular affection.

In turning to a consideration of the carol (and some loosely related topics) it is important to remember the partial eclipse of Christmas hymns like 'It came upon the midnight clear' by carols like 'Ding dong merrily on High'—and the part played by the schools in establishing this change. Of course the carol is very much associated with that movement in the Church of England and also beyond its boundaries which from small stirrings in the 1840's linked itself to Anglo-Catholic mediaevalism and to the resuscitation of national folk-song by Cecil Sharp, Vaughan Williams and their collaborators. This eventually gained enormous influence in the schools, not at all in terms of Anglo-Catholic doctrine (which has no extensive popular root whatever) but in terms of an evocation of rural England.

The schools, (whether under direct state or partial religious control), are important not only with regard to the folk-song revival but simply as the most important source of religious teaching. Outside the 'public schools' the parson is important largely because he presides over rites of passage: the central figure for teaching Christianity is a lady in a primary school. By a happy chance for Christianity those who teach in primary schools are amongst the most well-disposed to the faith and most strongly practising of all social strata. Their place as religious educators is very little disputed outside the ranks of the intelligentsia, and is a major reason why religion is regarded as 'a good thing' and the right way to keep the young on a decent path.

Although the instruction given reflects an element of mediaeval and rural nostalgia at the level of carols and plays, yet with regard to religious teaching and attitude it is profoundly Protestant. This is one reason (whatever the Established Church may do) why the teaching diffused by schools ensures an almost universal popular Protestantism, at least at the level of a preference for 'decency' as distinct from mere forms and practices, and a veneration for the person of Christ. Moreover, although the teachers are often devout Christians, they maintain a long tradition of resentment at parsonic interference, deriving from the time when clergy were more important in the control of schools than they are now. Ecclesiasticism has little foothold in the material passed on to children by the contemporary school.

But if ecclesiasticism has little influence, the *idea* of the Church remains very potent. It is linked with the whole sequence of national festivity associated with Christmas and also with the enormous interest aroused by liturgical celebrations like the Coronation. People are deeply attached to the sound of organs and boys' voices and feel a sense of relief grounded in traditional continuity that the cathedral spire and church tower still dominate the skyline.

To the Leftist section of the intelligentsia the Coronation may appear an expensive charade compounded by mediaeval gibberish, but to the British population at large it is one of the central forms of legitimization. The archbishop becomes the temporary and formal custodian of authority in the name of God, which he then 'gives back' to the monarch, just as 'the people' at a general election becomes temporary and formal custodian of a political power which it then gives back to Parliament. This church legitimization is highly characteristic of all the interlocking pluralisms which contribute to the stability of

British society, and it extends to the very lowest social strata in a way the somewhat more sophisticated sentiments mentioned above do not. On the one hand there is a populist check through the ballot on the concept of unrestricted sovereignty, balanced on the other hand by a check in terms of divine limits set to any form of power whatever. Whether framed in terms of natural law or the right to change the powers that be, or the pre-eminence of conscience, these notions are absolutely fundamental in British society in a manner scarcely paralleled anywhere else.

England: The Local Situation

The local situation can most easily be illustrated from two of the best community studies recently published: Margaret Stacey's study of Banbury and Williams' work on a Cumberland village—Gosforth.[4]

Mrs Stacey divided Banbury into four social 'connections': the Trade Union/Labour connection, the Free Church/friendly society/Liberal connection, and the upper and lower halves of the Conservative/Anglican/charitable body connection. These were then related to the traditional elements in society, centred on the older static professions, and to the non-traditional elements, based on the newer, more mobile professions and on workers, many of them migrant, who no longer accepted a situation of deference.

The connection focused on the Anglican Church and the Conservative Party had much the widest range of social contacts and attracted the greatest social prestige. This wide range of contacts divided into two segments even with respect to the important aspect of sport. The bowls clubs for example were divided into two parts, the upper consisting of a link between the parish church and the Chestnut Bowling Club, and the lower connecting the British Legion, the Conservative Club and the 'Borough Bowls'. The same division was repeated in other sports: the rugger, the tennis, the cricket and the hunting, which served to bring the larger farmers into contact with professional and business men, and the table-tennis league, the second cricket

---

[4] M. Stacey, *Tradition and Change: a Study of Banbury*, and W. M. Williams, *Gosforth. The Sociology of an English Village*.

club, the Post Office sports, etc. in which the 'deferentials' were normally expected to associate together.

The Free Church connection still maintained important links with the Liberal Party and had more interest in mutual help and education than in sport. To some extent it shared a frontier with the Anglican connection on the side of voluntary bodies. The older divisions between tradespeople who were Wesleyans and the artisan Primitive Methodists still existed to some extent, but the democratic ethos prevented this forming the kind of divide noted in the Anglican connection, although the central Methodist church tended to be the place where the nonconformist *élite* met to worship. The major meeting point between the two connections was the Rotary Club.

As for the Trade Union/Labour association, it was culturally isolated, but this isolation did not extend to the political sphere. Moreover, it contained those migrants and others who not only rejected the system of deference but also were comparatively less frequent in their religious practice. Practically all acknowledged some denomination. Whether people were active or passive members of this political-social axis they were notably inactive in *all* forms of other association, not merely the religious. This Banbury finding parallels identical findings for the same groupings in the London suburb of Woodford.[5]

So far as the churches themselves are concerned, it is interesting that the high status persons who call themselves Church of England and who regard it as 'their' church are usually dormant in their practice. Nevertheless, the church congregations faithfully reflect the class system. St Mary's, the parish church, attracts virtually all worshippers in the three highest status groups, regardless of where they live. St Mary's is not confined to these status groups; but the other churches certainly are confined in their social catchment area, so that Christ Church, for example, is almostly entirely artisan. The same structure is also reflected in the country churches, where the owner of the great house probably reads the lessons, where the seating arrangements place the gentry in front and others behind, and where the pattern of leadership in voluntary associations (especially those for women) firmly reflects the traditional status system.

[5] P. Willmott and M. Young, *Family and Class in a London Suburb.*

This pattern of leadership is just as plain in the voluntary associations described by Williams in Gosforth. No association is capable of flourishing unless patronized by a group known as the 'top ten'. But the alternative connections found in Banbury are largely absent in Gosforth: the Free Churches in Cumberland are mainly confined to the towns, and there is no avenue of escape from the enveloping system of social placement. This does not mean of course that the Anglican Church is extensively patronized. The church is important only at crucial turning points in the life cycle, or else where a secular festival overlaps an ecclesiastical one. Thus Whit Sunday is locally associated with the institution of club walks, and even Easter is the time when women appear in church in new clothes. Confirmation is the usual climax to the most intensive period of religious activity and once the rite has been administered church-going normally becomes increasingly rare. Somewhat oddly, this situation of indifference to religious duties is regarded as dating from the arrival of the present rector, when in fact it can be substantiated at least for the past 400 years and illustrates the continuing effects in some country areas of plural livings and long-term ecclesiastical neglect.

Wales: The Established Dissidence

We turn now to the issues raised by the pattern of religion in Wales. The English pattern has been described only very partially at the national and local level but the broad outlines are nevertheless clear enough and there is no reason to suppose that any part of England provides a substantial exception. Wales however is an exception. The Anglican Church in Wales remains the largest single denomination but it is definitely a minority. The connection of a (one-time) established church with a conservative party has been made an entirely subsidiary part of Welsh national life. Indeed, conservatism amongst the Welsh attracts the allegiance of a smaller minority than the church does, so that if Wales had an independent Parliament it would consist almost entirely of Socialists and Liberals.

The position can be summarized by comparison with the three systems of social life described in Banbury. The two subsidiary systems of Banbury move to the centre, and the central system moves to the periphery. In the industrial towns the main axis turns around a balance achieved between the Free Churches and the Trade Union/Labour Party connection; in the smaller country towns, villages and farms the Free Church/Liberal Party axis is dominant. Both connections are eroded at the edges and overlap each other, but this generalization is the simplest brief approximation to the facts.

The result has been that religious practice has never been associated with making adjustments to a social hierarchy but with the effort to express freedom from that hierarchy. Moreover, this effort, whether in industrial or rural areas, brought about a subtle interpenetration of national identity and dissenting religion which made piety a vigorous symbol of Welsh nationality. In these circumstances the fact of class did not make the kind of division within the society which could become a psychological barrier to the practice of religion. Moreover, certain aspects of the type of religion itself were specially suited to an industrial working class and those aspects which were ideologically out of tune with the eventual triumph of socialism were not placed in any structural opposition to it. Thus an adjustment was made without any fatal strains occurring. If any fatal strains are present now they derive from certain processes of mobility and Anglicization. These are fraying the pattern somewhat, partly because of the usual effects of urbanization in terms of alternative sources of leisure and entertainment, but partly also because nonconformist religion has acquired a degree of particularity in relation to the local structures of kin which is very easily corroded by extensive and continuous geographical mobility.[6]

This raises some points with regard to the notions of church, denomination and sect utilized by sociologists, since in Wales we see developed an interesting mixed case. The case is worth some discussion before we turn to the question of how it arose and the precise social forms and processes with which it was connected.

Plainly the type of religion is mainly of that democratic variety which originally had a largely urban root in England and which bases itself more on adult conviction than birthright member-

[6] See C. C. Harris, 'Church, Chapel and the Welsh' in *New Society*, 21 February, 1963.

ship. This democratic (or denominational) religion has normally avoided any prolonged or extensive connection with the total social system in a given area, apart from some exceptions in the colonial phase of American history. Yet, in Wales it *is* fairly coextensive with the social system on a territorial basis, and, apart from periods of revival, has developed birthright membership, or membership which is automatic enough on achieving adolescence to count practically as a birthright. At the same time this characteristic, normally associated with 'churches', has oscillated in times of revival (such as 1859 and 1904) with a degree of exclusiveness resting on the distinction between the saved and the 'hearers' which almost approximates the sociological definition of sect. Indeed, as examples will indicate, this distinction, originally set up in situations of religious dominance and fervour, can become fossilized into the major 'secular' differential within the social system at large. Let us now consider the evolution of this religion over time, first in the rural and then in the industrial regions.

The older 'dry dissent' made relatively little impact on Wales. Not only was it hampered by English associations but such roots as it struck were in the middle class and even some sections of the minor gentry.[7] The great change, so far as rural Wales was concerned, came in the eighteenth century. The Calvinistic or Wesleyan Methodists, and the older dissenters, now revitalized by evangelical zeal, spread with great rapidity, some achieving dominance in one area, some in another.

It seems that it was less the poorest who responded first than the artisan, the yeomen and the shopkeeper: people with some degree of freedom from the sanctions available against social or religious dissent by an older social system dominated by church and gentry.[8] Maybe there always was a poorer stratum who either did not respond to the new chapels or who because the less 'respectable' and less pious sections within the chapel community. The situation may have varied throughout the country, but it is at least evident that the gentry became isolated by the new

[7] This point I draw, along with the general historical background for South Wales, from E. T. Davies, *Religion in the Industrial Revolution in South Wales*, University of Wales Press, 1965.

[8] Cf. E. Davies and A. D. Rees, *Welsh Rural Communities*, University of Wales Press, 1960; note 47 to the section dealing with Aberdaron.

developments and that even those who adhered to the Established Church participated in the new changing values brought about by nonconformity.[9]

These values were partly those of a vigorous independence which replaced rural apathy, of mutual assistance through the chapels and of combined resistance to landlordism and the English. The political issues which arose from this confrontation were land reform, political and civil liberties, and also the disestablishment of the Church as a symbolic focus of ethnic and economic oppression. The cultural emphases which followed from the new religion rested on a greater importance attached to educational attainment than to sport, and a discipline in work which eliminated most entertainment not directly or indirectly connected with it. Cock-fighting disappeared, and the tavern remained only on sufferance, whereas sheep-shearing festivities and the agricultural fair maintained themselves. The Puritan spirit showed itself in Sunday observance, originally more positive in intention than now, in zeal for Sunday Schools (which included adults), in temperance and the rejection of gambling. Gambling became reprehensible because although the fruits of a man's honest labour and talent may be 'blessed', a fortuitous win is no incentive to industry or example of virtue.

It is important to observe how the decentralized structure of most nonconformist bodies fitted the decentralized familism of the Welsh countryside. Initially devotional meetings were linked to the economic and recreational gatherings occurring in rural farmsteads where domestic industry was carried on. Gradually the chapels took over these recreational gatherings and shifted the focus of local life to themselves.

In the larger centres they eventually reproduced certain forms of social differentiation recently derived from English urbanism: an occupational prestige system based on a preference for intellectual labour (the clerk, minister and professional man) as compared with manual labour. Even the chapel arrangements reflected this prestige hierarchy: the 'big seat' at the front for the diaconate and a gradation from centre to sides, with the

---

[9] I. Emmett says this is the case as regards the village which she studied in North Wales, but according to R. Frankenberg the values of the two groups are noticeably different; see his *Village on the Border,* Cohen and West, 1957.

gallery carrying least prestige of all.[10] But the basic egalitarian spirit was not eroded and a proliferation of minor offices or opportunities in connection with the organization of events like singing festivals ensured general participation. In filling offices outside the diaconate a moderately devout person might become a 'good man in the chapel' without necessarily being a 'good man on his knees'.

The spread of nonconformity meant that the division of society into members and 'hearers' collapsed into an internal distinction within the chapel broadly co-extensive with the respectable and the not quite so respectable. The respectable kept the chapel going, were willing to 'offer prayer' and placed more value on thrift, house ownership and education. These attitudes were transmitted through the family along with denominational affiliation and were kept in being by the sanction of 'family reputation'. However the aspirations of the respectable nowadays lead to a greater degree of migration, so that the leadership of the community is likely to suffer losses by migration to the large towns of England, and the community activities are simultaneously weakened.

The industrial situation developed somewhat differently. Nonconformity moved into the new industrial areas of South Wales along with the rural migrants and there acquired an urban working-class character. Once again the Welsh faced the English: partly in the form of a dominant church which only understood the relationship of squire and tenant and partly in the form of the owners of capital in the new industries. In this situation teetotalism[11] became a tactic against the improvidence and drunkenness which some masters actually encouraged. In-

---

[10] Cf. E. Davies and A. D. Rees, *op. cit.*; section dealing with Tregaron.

[11] It is worth remembering that the association of nonconformists with the teetotal section of the temperance movement is only a little over a century old. There was a time when a man found it difficult to enter the Methodist ministry because he was teetotal, rather than the reverse.

Unfortunately so far as I know we lack a sociological account of the temperance movement in Britain. Joseph Gusfield has provided such an account for America in his *Symbolic Crusade*, 1966, which links the movement to the status anxieties of native and rural Protestants under urban Catholic (or secular) pressure. So far as Britain is concerned a perusal of almost any biography dealing with early Labour politicians reveals a strong connection with the temperance agitation.

deed, a kind of polarization developed between chapel and public house, with the former dominant in the frontier-style revivals which recurred up to 1859 and then again in 1904. Moreover, these revivals and the fervent preaching to be found even in normal periods made the chapels centres of theatrical excitement.

The chapels were not greatly concerned with social problems as distinct from the issues of civil liberties during the nineteenth century. They were certainly co-operative in ethos but their social critique stopped short of social arrangements, which were largely taken as beyond moralization. This made them initially unresponsive to socialism when it arrived, quite apart from its English taint and occasional secularism. But just as the Welsh had made 'dissent' their own so they eventually naturalized socialism, and became the most socialist region in the British Isles. By the first world war the shift was occurring on a large scale from Liberal politics explicitly based on the chapel to Labour politics supported by most chapel-going people and the occasional minister. The political split brought within nonconformity by the advent of Labour politics prevented any continuing explicit involvement of the chapels in political life.

Moreover, certain social developments had occurred which shifted segments of nonconformity upwards on the social scale and created a Welsh middle class. The first of these was the spreading dominance of the coal industry. Thrift, hard work and an apprenticeship in offices of responsibility brought Welshmen to higher positions in the coal industry, some as colliery managers, others even as a new group of Welsh capitalists. The kind of man who was colliery manager and chapel deacon became prominent; and the plain chapel building acquired neo-classical or neo-Gothic trimmings. Nonconformist traders and managers utilized the new educational opportunities then available, created a professional class and through it dominated the schools and local politics.[12] From this nonconformist urban middle class Welsh nationalist politics eventually drew substantial sections of its support.

The crucial developments, however, have been the creation of a Free Church/Trade Union axis and the erosion of nonconformity through English influences and through the effects of

[12] Cf. E. T. Davies, *op. cit.*

D

mobility and alternative social centres. What this latter has meant may be gauged from the fact that whereas church attendance on a Sunday in rural Wales may involve two-thirds or more of the population, in Swansea only about a quarter will be attending a place of worship on a given Sunday.

It will be obvious that the cultural isolation of the Labour Party and Trade Unions found in Banbury does not occur in South Wales. The compromise axis of Labour with the Free Church forms the hub of social life in local politics, government, education and voluntary association. The system is worth describing, partly because so much of the 'chapel' image of the Labour Party in fact derives from it, and partly because there are links with the wider Weber thesis concerning the propriety and adjustment of Protestant values to those of industrial civilization.

The chapels and trade unions as described by Brennan and his collaborators form a left to right grouping, whereby the 'hub' of the system turns on those who are leaders in the right wing unions and also in the 'left' wing chapels, notably the Congregationalists and Baptists.[13] These two denominations have over 50% working-class leadership. Together these union and chapel leaders dominate all politics, except those of the small Conservative Party where younger professionals and older business men predominate. It is noticeable that the Trade Union side of the axis leans towards the thrift societies, amenities and sports in its cultural leadership, whereas the chapel side leans towards choirs, music, temperance and the YMCA.

Four segments may be discerned, the outer two of which lie beyond the system and could be important for its future development. The first outer segment comprises a working class often to be found in the newer light industries, which is not very interested in either chapel or trade union and restricts its associational life to the family, personal groups, or perhaps the working-men's club. The second outer segment is found amongst an English or Anglicized middle class, largely without political consciousness, religiously dormant and with recreational interests (say) at the level of the Rotary or the golf club. At the centre of the system are the strongly Welsh working and middle class, the former

[13] The whole of this section leans heavily on T. Brennan, E. W. Cooney and M. Pollins, *Social Change in South-West Wales*, Watts, 1954.

consisting of skilled older men in the older basic industries, the latter of professional people, especially teachers, centred on the chapel or cultural and benevolent activities associated with it. Plainly this core of the pattern is threatened by the decline in Welsh-speaking, the new sources of entertainment and instruction outside the chapel, geographical mobility—and even, for chapel people, less fertility.[14] As young men no longer follow fathers into the old local industries the basis of continuity is threatened.

Finally, something might be said about the values of this society as they contrast with those of England. The combination of chapel with socialism and nationalism has produced an emphasis on peace as a value common to potentially rival loyalties. Another common value is brotherhood. Both these contrast strongly with the English pattern, where peace sentiment is more characteristic of the professional segment of the middle class and where hierarchy and status are absolutely fundamental. Similarly, the emphasis on thrift brings the Welsh working class closer to the English lower middle class and distinguishes both from the hedonism of the aristocracy and much of the English working class. Finally, the primacy of education as the basis of status allied to the prestige of public service is in partial contrast to England. English culture is somewhat suspicious of intelligence and simultaneously mistrustful of enthusiasm. Somewhat oddly the nonconformist tradition has given to Wales an admiration for both. That these differentials exist is some estimate of the role played by the shape of religious institutions in the broad moulding of national awareness and values.

[14] According to C. C. Harris and K. C. Rosser, *The Family and Social Change*, Routledge, 1965.

CHAPTER FIVE

Explanations

GENERAL explanations of the difficulties experienced by religious institutions in our society cannot be separated from classical approaches to the various cross-cutting developments encapsulated in the word secularisation.[1] These classical approaches are not in themselves simple empirical hypotheses but global proclamations, often of a mutually contradictory kind, which nevertheless contain elements of useful empirical analysis.

Broadly the vast variety of explanation can be brought under the umbrella of four basic 'proclamations'. Firstly there is a criticism of religion associated with Nietszche and Freud in which the superman challenges the superego. Secondly there is a criticism of religion advanced by Feuerbach and Marx whereby man claims God's powers and attributes as justly his own. These two traditions share a great deal in common: but they have a psychological and sociological basis respectively, signalized in the cognate terms 'rationalization' and 'ideology'. However, whereas the former sees 'society' and its legitimating ideologies as permanently repressive, the latter sees only particular forms of society as such, notably bourgeois capitalism.

The third and fourth approaches are not hostile to religion in the same way as the first two, though they are neither of them Christian. They are associated with Durkheim and with Weber, and instead of a proclamation of man's liberation from religion they see correlative dangers: either the domination of 'rational

---

[1] I have discussed the concept of secularization in 'Towards Eliminating the Concept of Secularisation', *Penguin Survey of the Social Sciences*, ed. J. Gould, 1965, and 'Some Utopian Elements in the Concept of Secularisation', *Internationales Jahrbuch für Religionsoziologie*, Westdeutscher Verlag, Köln and Opladen, 1966.

bureaucracy', or else a pathological isolation as the increasing division of labour disintegrates society and religion along with it. Both these approaches regard religion as protecting man's self-hood within society rather than repressing it. Yet neither holds out much hope for Christianity. Durkheim sees man as perhaps reintegrated through a faith in the idealized society (nationalism for example), while Weber sees the advance of science and of bureaucracy initiating a progressive dissolution of the myths which veil nature and the social reality.[2]

No attempt will be made to give any general assessment or lengthy exposition of these positions. They are simply spring-boards from which to initiate discussion of various aspects of British society coming within their ambit of concern. Durkheim's emphasis on problems of social disintegration for example provides a useful lead into a consideration of the effects of several different kinds of mobility. Similarly the Marxist concentration on class allows comment on the special character of the cultural distinctions found in Britain.

Using the fourfold classification we need not spend much time on the first. The reason is quite simple: if the role of religion in validating repressive social rules and institutions is semi-permanent, then an analysis which utilizes such a framework does not explain particular changes. It simply proclaims a possibility of liberation open to a privileged few: either the Freudian 'ethic of honesty' or the existential 'ethic of authenticity'. The statement that God is dead refers to a private death in the psyche of a minority. For this minority the sons have replaced the fathers and the condemned criminals have taken the place of the righteous judges: they have, if you like, seen the inner significance of Christianity itself as a sceptical rather than a validatory religion. Of course, there are some 'optimists' who believe that this scepticism can evangelize, but immediately the process of evangelization appears to begin it is transformed in a manner more spiritually disastrous even than the develop-ment of primitive Christianity under Constantine. It becomes an ethic of 'adjustment' in which the human judges and fathers cannot even be challenged by the divine fatherhood or the judge-

[2] E. Durkheim, *Elementary Forms of Religious Life*, Allen and Unwin, 1957.

ment of God. Optimistic atheisms always invite their own self-destruction.

Nevertheless it can be argued that the secret is 'out' and that spectacles exist for people to see that emperors and priests really do have no clothes. And it is doubtless true that authority can less easily validate itself simply by being 'authority', and has to pretend to be *an* authority'—an expert. Thus oppression and repression need to utilize quasi-scientific myths and to talk in an apparently empirical way. The old symbols remain immensely powerful, but they are locked together with a promise to produce the benefits of modern technology quicker than other alternatives.[3] For example conservatism nowadays never explicitly appeals to the royal descent from Adam (as Filmer did in the seventeenth century) or to the fact that divine providence has set the nation in various social degrees which cannot be ignored without cosmic disaster.[4] It simply says that conservatism works.

Marxism is an optimistic atheism which has encountered the dangers of perversion just referred to, but because it is optimistic it also has a doctrine of social change and this includes some analysis of the role of religion in the 'interim' period of capitalism. It regards capitalism as utilitarian and worldly insofar as it develops techniques for mundane objectives, but also as destroying the web of mutual involvement between man and master and man and craft. These involvements are depersonalized and the whole economic world subject to forces which are arbitrary and which control capitalist and worker alike. Hence the capitalist period is contrasted with the previous era of feudalism: capitalism destroys the control of religion over economic life as well as eroding all idyllic, feudal, patriarchal relations. It substitutes the cash nexus.

Initially capitalism challenges religion in the name of rationality and then utilizes it as the opiate of the people. In the bourgeois period religion is a fantastic hope either of heaven on earth or of heaven after death. Either way it can only be a pre-

---

[3] Ernest Gellner has discussed this question at length in *Thought and Change*, Weidenfeld and Nicolson, 1964.
[4] Cf. P. Laslett, Introduction to Filmer's *Patriarcha* (and other works), Blackwell, 1949.

lude to a scientific socialism which will progressively inform the consciousness of the workers. Eventually both religious 'mediation' (the Church, Christ) or bourgeois mediation (the state) will give way to a clear awareness of reality through which workers will perceive their 'true' rational interests in revolution.

Put crudely, this analysis fits Catholic countries better than Protestant countries insofar as the separation of society into two warring camps with religion largely on one side has been fairly characteristic of Catholic countries up to the first half of the twentieth century. It fits neither insofar as Protestant countries have been more advanced but less revolutionary and (in an institutional form) less 'religious' than Catholic countries. Thus in Protestant countries the decline of religious institutions has gone hand in hand with the decline of any revolutionary possibility and *not* with the near onset of revolution. Moreover it has been the middle and not the working classes who have been addicted to their own opiates. In almost every crucial respect the Marxist theory of religion finds England a most unhappy example.[5]

Yet, whereas few people still take the Freudian theory of religion seriously, the Marxist theory remains suggestive and important. The destruction of intimate master and man relationships and ties between squire and farm labourer did indeed have profound consequences, but, in England, for various reasons connected with a pre-existing tradition of dissenting religion and the progressive institutionalization of pragmatic reform, the expected split into two warring political camps did not occur. Instead, there appeared two (or more) mutually incomprehensible cultures. Politically the working class either embraced reformism or maintained attitudes of deference. Even its reformism had limited mundane objectives. Only segments of the professional middle class showed signs of socialist consciousness, apart that is from one or two areas of Britain where working-class ethnic groups like Jews, Welsh and Scots-Irish had suffered extreme deprivation.[6]

---

[5] For Engels' discussion of England in the mid-nineteenth century cf. H. Desroches, *Socialisme et sociologie religieuse*, Editions Cujas, Paris, 1964.

[6] Cf. R. T. McKenzie and A. Silver, 'Conservatism, Industrialism and the Working-class Tory in England', Fifth World Congress of the International Sociological Association, Washington, 1962.

The English working class remains one of the most unrevolutionary and one of the most irreligious in the world.[7] As we have seen it 'believes' in Christianity after a fashion, but it will be enticed into church only with great difficulty. That is why one must rely on an explanation based on the cultural rather than the political chasms.

We are, welfare state and short-distance social mobility notwithstanding, one of the most minutely stratified and status-conscious of peoples. The prime basis of this status differentiation is not so much money (as in the American class system) as style of life and the most important single focus of it all is gesture and voice. 'Them' and 'us' are distinguished by enunciation. Of course one of the functions of higher education is to pass on this enunciation, and to the extent that clergy participate in such education they tend to acquire the appropriate class stigmata. If they are Anglican they probably possessed such stigmata from birth. The effect is to mark off the church as a class institution and to secure an uninterested respect for pronouncements made in the correct manner. Any clergyman who rejects the vocal mark of status will run the risk of seeming out of place and lacking in authority: a problem which may well become quite unpleasant if the class recruitment of Anglican clergy continues to fall.

The importance of 'the voice' is indicated in a small but significant way by the finding of an investigation into the popularity of American films, which suggested that working-class cinema-goers were unwilling to put up with the purest tones of English establishment enunciation bleating at them from the screen. This creates special difficulties for the churches: priests feel a need to make contact in a way other professions do not and yet specialized priestly modes of speaking are more than normally frequent. In the case of Anglicanism not merely is the manner characteristic of a contemporary class culture but the *matter* is characteristic of a gentry culture some three or four centuries ago. The seventeenth-century ideals of restraint and impersonality are not those of modern working-class life nor are they even related to the sentimentalities of lower-middle-class

---

[7] W. G. Runciman has a useful discussion of the working classes' apathy on their own behalf in *Relative Deprivation and Social Justice*, Routledge, 1966.

styles. To that extent the Anglican liturgy is a refuge for the aesthetically sensitive.

The implications of this are that far too much can be made of the reactionary *political* stance of the Church of England in the alienation of the working classes during the nineteenth century. In any case the penetration of progressive ideas through the professional segments of the upper middle class ensures that nowadays the attitudes (as distinct from the identifications) of higher clergy are often well to the left of the working class. What we have now are cultural identifications maintained in part by the enormous inertia of habit. Something of the extraordinary power of this inertia can be grasped by the fact that atypical and favourable attitudes towards the Church of England set up in the 1830's and 1840's in north-west England can be shown to persist to the present day.[8]

One aspect of working-class styles especially important for participation in church life is the widespread resistance to *any* kind of major involvement in voluntary associations, trade unions included. With every step up the status scale active participation in voluntary associations of every kind increases. These are somewhat differently distributed as between the churches themselves: the Free Churches maintain their own integrated network of association whereas the Church of England is uniquely linked with a number of generally available associations, often of a charitable kind, usually run by high status persons, such as upper-middle-class women.[9] By contrast the working-class style is based on kin and neighbourhood and only emerges for the pub, the cinema and the football match. Indeed, so far as women are concerned not even this minimal emergence is likely.[10]

This is an appropriate point at which to transfer discussion to the sort of concerns initiated by the work of Durkheim and his contemporary Tönnies. One of the distinctions most widely employed by sociologists is the contrast between community and

[8] A. H. Birch, *Small Town Politics.*

[9] See Rosalind Chambers' contribution to D. V. Glass (ed.), *Social Mobility in Britain*, Routledge, 1954.

[10] Documentation is available in Cauter and Downham, *The Communication of Ideas*, and H. Gavron, *The Captive Wife*, Routledge, 1966.

D*

association, (*Gemeinschaft* and *Gesellschaft*).[11] Broadly the former refers to close, stable, local, 'all in' relationships while the latter refers to groups formed for particular purposes in which relations tend to be tangential and also tend to provide the participant with only one of several other roles which he plays in different contexts. The proliferation of these associational forms is usually related to the vast increase in the scale, complexity and structural differentiation of modern society based on the division of labour.

In the communal type of society religion is the mainspring of the common life in that it forms the everyday secular focus of most activities. It provides the controlling sanctions and norms, which are recognized even when they are ignored. It is often supposed therefore that the contemporary churches are communal groupings trying to maintain themselves in an associational society: the diminished and diminishing hub of a vanished common life of which the church building remains the last visible symbol.

Yet modern churches are clearly middle- and lower-middle-class associations providing one tangential relationship among others—and that not perhaps the most important. They are the religious variety of club for the clubbable classes. Paradoxically however the common and public aspect of the churches' existence maintains itself at the level of widespread perceptions of religion. Religion or 'Christianity' is *still* what unites us: the umbrella identification. Just because we are a highly differentiated society in which each group has conflicting interests and psychologies we cannot physically mix in churches (beyond a certain range of social status) and yet require the word 'Christian' and visible symbol of the church spire to symbolize our common membership in the same society. That is why the social action of the churches must be restricted to certain agreed humane objectives which do not raise the crucial dividing issues within or outside religious bodies, or to the public rhetoric of unity and social harmony which nobody takes seriously except in relation to the disputes of other people.

---

[11] For ways in which these are used see P. Mann, *An Approach to Urban Sociology*, Routledge, 1965, and R. Frankenberg, *Communities in Britain*, Pelican, 1966.

Thus the Durkheimian analysis of religion as the focus of common identity remains more appropriate than ever. Religion provides the obfuscating but necessary rhetoric of public harmony. Stranger still, this reaches its climax in Britain with a coronation ceremony in which apparent and latent functions are widely separated. Formally the coronation is a symbol of the stable, sacral society; latently it is a symbol of a community *without consensus*. Some sociologists have suggested that the coronation is important because we have consensus.[12] The reverse is true: the extraordinary *éclat* of such an occasion arises because common identifications have to fill in the chasm left by the non-existence of cultural consensus or the common life. No wonder the Crown and Christianity need to be put beyond politics, and no wonder violent reactions occur whenever Christianity steps outside either agreed humanities or ritual appeals for an end to social strife such as bishops are supposed to make every time a non-professional group endeavours to improve its position.

There are two aspects of the traditional notion of *Gemeinschaft* which require further comment because they bear on British religious patterns: localism and stability. Much of the work done recently on English working-class life suggests that it exhibits those elements of *Gemeinschaft* which are still extant in our society. To the extent that this is true, proletarian communalism does not revolve around any common religious institution. Indeed it might be possible to say that working-class cultures are *Gemeinschaften* without religion, whereas in middle-class cultures religion is one *Gesellschaft* amongst many. But in any case the traditional close-knit working-class area of the cotton towns, East London, Huddersfield and so on, is less in evidence today and a more mobile pattern of living exists for many working-class groups: the workers in the motor industry, for example. Of course some industries like building have been traditionally mobile. Maybe the Bethnal Greens always were infrequent and working-class mobility always fairly marked, at least from one generation to another.

The point of this analysis is simply to enquire about the effects

[12] M. Young and E. Shils, 'The Meaning of the Coronation', *Sociological Review* 1 (2), Dec. 1953.

of contemporary mobility on different class ways of life. As the pattern of close-knit relations and neighbourly sanctions is eroded the group solidarity of working-class people against religious practice could also be weakened, just as the group solidarity of the village is weakened in the reverse direction. So far as the village is concerned of course one is less and less confronted by the organic community and more and more by the commuter dormitory or haven for the retired. But it is the middle-class suburban pattern of short-period mobility which is of especial interest because it undergoes continuous expansion and might for a number of reasons exist in some tension with relatively high institutional practice.

However, having indicated varying points of concern with respect to different class, status and regional styles it may be as well to simply discuss the mobility of our society in general, bearing in mind from time to time how it may affect the various *milieux* mentioned. It is necessary to begin by suggesting the different forms of mobility which will be relevant to our enquiry. There is first the simple fact of rapid social change. Then there is geographical and social mobility: movement from one place to another on business or at the call of one's profession and movement from one status grouping to another. Finally there are the kinds of mobility more directly dependent on technological progress: the impact in particular of the car in allowing physical movement for leisure pursuits, and the impact of mass media. This last—the mass media—results in a combination of perceptual mobility with physical immobility. To put it epigrammatically: the modern Briton is either mobile in his car or immobile in front of his television.

Take, to begin with, the impact of rapid change. Just as in the world of science the firm world of substance and eternal law has dissolved in favour of dynamic activity and expanding pragmatic possibilities, so the firm patterns of the social and moral cosmos enter a similar condition of flux. The motor car as a contemporary symbol of obsolescence and expendability does not exactly convey a sense of eternal verities. The cyclical rhythms of the natural world to which the liturgical rhythms of the church are partly geared give way to a variable, fragmented, adjustable urban regularity. In such a context the main function of the church is all too easily confined to rural nostalgias, and to the sanctification of threatened habits and the evocation of cosmic securities. Indeed, there is plenty of evidence that for many people the church acts as the still point in a turning world.

This is not necessarily bad, since the human being collapses without points of reference or when deprived of social continuities, but the problem of relevance requires the church to find a way to link the horizontal and vertical planes of its existence in a way not so far remotely achieved. All the contemporary church appears able to do is to validate local *mores*, prejudices and assumptions just at the point when these are in visible flux. The consequence must be that the point of reference is seen to hobble belatedly after the points of change, in spite of the sophistication evident in some recent commissions and in reports from expert boards of social responsibility and Christian citizenship.

This is one of the reasons why many people are grateful for the existence of the church so long as they are not brought close enough to share in its confusions. It is very moving to listen to the voices of hidden choirs provided one is not also involved in a dispute about methods of birth control. The plagal cadence is splendid when overheard by accident. This is why sensitive contemporary persons restrict their religious awareness to the pure symbolism of the concert hall instead of facing the legitimate confusions of social relevance to which the church is half-committed.[13] Happily Bach is not problematic.

Short-term occupational mobility, either in the sense of having a network of professional or business connections over a wide area or moving one's place of work every three or four years is very much a middle-class pattern. It is found in what Frank Musgrove has called 'the migratory *élite*'.[14] For such people life is tightly geared to career requirements which dominate their private almost as much as their vocational existence. The older style of the professional man, say the doctor or lawyer, exercising long-term responsibilities to a local community is increasingly uncharacteristic of the newer professions. The scale and pace of operations are greatly increased.

---

[13] Colleagues tell me that they enjoy church atmosphere and music but are repelled by the content of sermons.

[14] F. Musgrove, *The Migratory Elite*, Heinemann, 1963.

Unfortunately no studies have been done of the impact of the newer professional styles on patterns of local responsibility and religious practice, but on the face of it considerable differences ought to exist. Engineers, for example, are subject to professional, not local, concerns and sanctions. Movement at short notice can hardly assist any local roots or religious participation, unless the church is seen as the universal association which can provide one's point of contact wherever one moves. Free Churchmen do in fact sometimes feel like this. Yet this seems the less likely development since most of our evidence suggests the importance of long-standing personal contacts in maintaining church practice: once people move, either at late adolescence or in the course of pursuing a career the new church is never 'quite the same'. Moreover, they are sometimes very glad to drop the burden of responsibilities which an over-strained home church has placed on the few available shoulders.[15]

Movements of population are not simply individually motivated but occur in response to market factors and government policy. The flight to the suburbs remains also a flight of the churches. Generally this means full suburban churches (partly) because these are few enough to meet demand whereas the churches in the older areas are like beautiful hulks resting on mud banks from which the main channels of life have long since flowed elsewhere: unless, that is, they are able to utilize the separation of workplace from home by providing services or guild facilities for the city centre during the week.

Social mobility, in the sense of shifts of status, has a varying impact on church practice. For those who shift into the lower middle class, particularly the expanding white-collar and clerical occupations, it may mean that marginality is one factor in the kind of aspiration which includes church-going in its definition of respectability. Alternatively it may also be that upper-working-class homes exposed to the norms of church people (perhaps through the mother) are differentially mobile compared to those who are not exposed. This kind of process operates in the sphere

---

[15] William Pickering traces reasons for dropping or taking up the habit of church-going (as well as analysing inter-church exchanges) in 'Religious Movements of Church Members in two Working Class Towns in England', *Archives de Sociologie des Religions* 11, Jan.-June 1961.

of education and it would be surprising if church practice were quite unrelated to it.[16] Certainly one suspects that a process of collective denominational social mobility occurs in the Free Churches, though the point would be very difficult to prove in a situation where the new professions and positions provide a wide range of expanded opportunities theoretically open to all.

Mobility at a higher level however can even erode church attachments. Partly it is the effect of acquaintance with different ways of life and the relativization of standards which may derive from such acquaintance. Partly also it is the making of contacts, from professional co-operation to marriage, where what is specific to oneself needs to be played down in favour of the common ground. But so far as the university educated are concerned there is also contact with the donnish religion of humanism, either in its winesmanship guise or in the form of the highly-sensitized middle-class conscience. These somewhat unrelated variations on a humanist theme are quite widespread in certain segments of the 'creative' upper professional groupings, who certainly identify church-going with the somewhat stuffy world of a despised commercial middle class.[17] One suspects that Roman Catholics are partly shielded from these challenges by a slower rate of mobility and proportional under-representation in the universities. The reverse is probably true of the unusually mobile and educationally aspiring Jewish community.

Physical mobility in Britain is important for our purposes because of its connection with the vastly expanded facilities for leisure and for making contacts, particularly in large cities. Visiting relations, watching sports, going away for the weekend: all these are made easier by the possession of a car. The institutions of Sunday church and Sunday School as well as weekday activities must contend with all the modern alternative avenues for enjoyment and interest. It is in response to these pressures that the Roman Catholic view of Sunday and timing of services is more flexible than evangelical Sabbatarianism or the Free

[16] Cf. B. Jackson and D. Marsden, *Education and the Working Class*, Routledge, 1962.

[17] For an analysis of the membership of the British Humanist Society see an article by C. B. Campbell in the *Sociological Review* 13 (3), Nov. 1965.

Church belief that the divine presence can only be entered punctually at eleven o'clock and six-thirty.

This physical activity contrasts sharply with the passivity induced by the mass media. Passive participation has been discussed *ad nauseam* but nevertheless it exists and it does affect attitudes to church attendance. Moreover, the standards of mass entertainment introduce a new dimension of technical achievement (as distinct from quality of content) with which the churches hardly compete. Certainly the possession of a television is marginally related to decline in active church participation. At the same time this passivity includes a great deal of home listening and home viewing of religious services. In this respect the churches simply suffer along with sport and every other form of organized activity from the universal availability of television and wireless within the home.

The preceding discussion has been focused on the role of institutions concerned with the common life and the symbolic representation of group values in a society increasingly differentiated, segmented and mobile in every sense. The primary agent in this process has been the scientific and technological revolution and we need therefore to conclude this general survey by a discussion of certain more specific effects of that revolution on religious practice and awareness. The convenient focus here is the work of Weber, notably his conception of rationalization as the fundamental process of social development. Whereas Freud sees this development in terms of a recapitulation of the maturational process and its repressions, Marx in terms of class war dynamics, and Durkheim in terms of progressive differentiation, for Weber the core concept is rationalization—or disenchantment.

Weber was concerned to show the increasing importance of the type of social action based on the most efficient technical achievement of mundane ends. This importance was to some extent at the expense of the psychological efficiency and rational effort which religion dedicated to the achievement of transcendental objectives. Thus the intellectual disciplines of Thomism and the taut psychology of Calvinism formed an essential preparation for the modern world. The godly discipline of the Presbytery became transmuted into the godless work disciplines of the industrial and scientific revolutions. Thus both of these key pro-

cesses were pregnant with developments stronger than themselves
and were to be corroded by their own potentialities.

Rationality has never been so important in Britain as in France
but the Calvinist psychological deposit has been always with us.
Moreover the Calvinist matter-of-fact attitude to Nature has also
been of importance in breaking through the rhythms and en-
chantments of the material world and establishing a neutral,
scientific attitude. To some extent this emotional break with
Nature can even be regarded as a Jewish achievement come to
late fruition through Calvinist agency.

Whatever the precise role of Calvinism in breaking certain
crucial taboos (and there has of course been vast debate over the
question[18]) there is no doubt about the process of rationalization
in the sphere of procedures and with respect to the emotional
blick which men have of the material and social worlds. Certainly we retain basic metaphysical assumptions underlying our
scientific activity and subscribe to potent social myths, but these
myths are at least rationalistic in form. Moreover, it is clear that
the sphere of the quantifiable has been greatly extended, and
many aspects of experience hitherto regarded as not amenable
to science shown as at least in part susceptible to it. (That the
social and psychological spheres in crucial respects are not
capable of assimilation to natural science procedures I would be
the last to deny.)

Put crudely and at the most general level it might be possible
to argue that what a secularized rationalism has been in French
life a pragmatic utilitarianism has been in British. The consequence is a comparative indifference to the contemplative, the
transcendent, the qualitative, the intrinsic and the sacred as
distinct from the quantitative and the instrumental. The assumption that everything can be bought is easily transmuted into the
assumption that most things can be measured. As a matter of
fact this type of easy analysis, which lines up sets of alternatives
and attributes one set or another to given historical periods or
nations is itself profoundly suspect, but it may still contain a
large enough residuum of truth to stimulate more precise state-

[18] For discussions, cf. L. S. Feuer, *The Scientific Intellectual*, Basic Books,
ᴇ964; and R. W. Greenlaw (general editor), *Problems in European Civilisation:*
vol. on *Protestantism and Capitalism*, ed. R. W. Green, Harrap, 1959.

ments of the changes which have actually occurred.

At any rate if the sacred or the divine is identified with the mysterious and unknowable, then what is conventionally mysterious is in principle steadily diminishing: the God of the gaps has increasingly few gaps to fill in our society or any other. Similarly, the God of contingency, the deity of the insurance man, has been placed at one or two removes from the modern consciousness. Contemporary Western man has his anxieties all right, but they are caused as much by relationships as by the omnipresence of death, accident and disease. Fewer and fewer people are willing to attribute the short-fall of human technical achievement to the divine limits set on the Promethean hubris. Some Christians even prefer to regard the recalcitrance of nature as equivalent to those demonic forces which the early Church claimed to have been vanquished by Christ.[19] The psychology which welcomed widespread destruction by floods in 1953 as a sign and symbol of God-given limits cannot but be on the wane. Similarly, disease and pain are no longer generally regarded as scourges for sin, at least at the conscious level. What happens at the psychosomatic level may be a different matter.

Yet here one wishes to interpose a query and a warning. Evidence already cited shows the prevalence of quasi-causal notions derived from superstition and magic as well as the extraordinary and continuing hold of certain kinds of social mythology. In many respects the doctrines of the Church are much more sophisticated than average thinking and the problem is too little education and not too much. It would be absurd to suppose that a population widely nurtured on the *Daily Express* and *Old Moore's Almanack* finds the New Testament an intellectual insult or Thomism not compatible with modern logic.

Indeed, technically sophisticated societies, America and Russia as well as ourselves, are capable of living by belief systems emotionally and intellectually crass to the point of nausea. The perverse transcendence of the American way of life, the cult of royalty or the threadbare eschatology and diseased vocabulary of Marxist aspiration is an index of the fantastic gullibility of modern man. This is because scientific learning is so specific

[19] John Wren-Lewis, for example.

that there is little carry-over outside the narrow sphere of immediate concern, not even so far as a general understanding of scientific procedures. It is left to the prejudices inculcated by humanist culture to create such generalized scepticism as manages to maintain itself in contemporary Britain. Even these prejudices are not genuinely understood so much as simply imbibed with the *New Statesman* as the appropriate atmosphere for those who aspire to be intellectual.

It could be, of course, that Wellsian dreams about science percolate through to the general mind just as the Rationalist Press once created a diffuse atmosphere of suspicious irreligion for the earnest artisan. Yet what seeps through is bastardized and magicked out of all recognition. If engineers do not understand the ethos of science and the rules of logical inference how should commercial travellers and estate agents understand them?

Moreover, there remains a perennial urge to fit the scientific achievement (and the scientific threat) into a framework of overall religious meaning such as vulgarized Marxism provides in communist countries. Perhaps in conclusion it will be useful to refer to two small movements which do indicate the existence of such an urge.[20] It could be claimed that such movements are merely the tip of the iceberg. Contemporary orthodox religion makes few attempts positively to incorporate scientific advance into a global system of understanding. But the Aetherius Society, with its mythical apparatus of visits to Mars and messages from planetary beings (latterly joined by Jesus himself) obviously does. It also provides a means of counteracting the technological threat of atomic disaster by a natural magnetism which is released by the systematic 'charging up' of mountains throughout the world. Similarly, scientology works at the level of a psychology which it utilizes to make its devotees masters of their own personal fate. The followers of scientology are processed until they become 'clears' or psychological and intellectual supermen. The movement even issues a degree: D.Sc., or Doctor of Scientology. The example is absurd but its import is serious. The movement of science tends to be placed within an average understanding of

---

[20] J. A. Jackson, 'Two Contemporary Cults', *Advancement of Science*, June 1966.

causality and inference popular before Christianity was thought of, while the extent and character of technical achievement produces a demand that it shall be set within a religious framework of meaning. A society ceases to provide such a framework at its peril.

CHAPTER SIX

What Needs to be Done:
Perspectives for Research

'Judgement' and the Facts

PART of the object of this book has been to show what we do not know about religion in Britain. It is no exaggeration to say that hundreds of social scientists could be employed on these problems and still leave the field unexhausted. As things are, some dozen or more expend their part-time energies on the sociology of religion, encountering the surprise of the sociological community and the suspicion of some sections of the churches. The result is that they expend not only their spare time but sometimes their spare money.

It would strike people as very curious if an industrial organization confronted by urgent development problems did almost nothing about them itself and was content for a few chemists to see what they could manage in their own time on their own money. But it would seem even more curious if that organization then complained that results were rather meagre and chemistry well-nigh useless. Unhappily that is sometimes not so far from the situation.

Of course, the churches are not industrial firms confronted with scientific problems nor sellers of brand peas requiring research to probe the market. The churches have, in any case, generally considered it more important to be, to do or even to think rather than to know. Yet thinking and Christian action do not occur in a vacuum: there is a factual context to action, and thinking cannot go on creatively by a mere extension of first principles. Indeed there is a social context to thinking; and it might be useful amongst other things to explore why people prefer thinking from first principles to empirical enquiry. The point is that logic and fact require each other and if principled action encounters particular kinds of limitation or encourages reactions actually damaging to wider purposes then the imperative which prescribes 'do this' at least needs re-examination. Christian witness cannot proceed by mere act of proclamation.

The offence which Christians rightly take to the commercial analogy turns partly on the pervasive association which it has with supply and demand criteria. It is all very well they might say to speak of a social and factual context, but ultimately the market must adjust to religion or to Christ, not *vice versa*. They would add that the Church has survived hitherto without the blandishments of ad-men and the advice of sociologists.

Yet precisely this ability to survive has been based on a capacity to adjust *de facto* while making formal reservations *de jure*. This applies not only in the sphere of the state, of power, and of *mores*, but in such 'smaller' matters as ecclesiastical provision in large cities. A parish of 100,000 souls in Stockholm for instance represented just such an accommodation of supply to demand, and it elicited an equivalent accommodation of demand to supply. Parishes of 20,000 in this country expressed the same basic principle. If you save resources by assembling large units simply because there seems little local need, then the local need diminishes even further.

A sociologist might well have warned *against* this particular accommodation to the market mechanism. He might also have suggested certain limitations in the actual notion of the territorial parish as a unit of evangelism. Certainly he could have provided information on the impact of different numerical ratios between clergy and population, and indicated viable areas of pastoral care. This is not simply the obvious and by now well-recognized point that if town-planners can study the basis of 'neighbourhood' groupings then they can also study the basis of the parish. The two need to be considered together. It is one of the special characteristics of sociology (as distinct say, from economics) that it is emasculated by being divided into compartments. And this is what might recommend it to those who practice the science of ecclesiastical administration: it rejects the conceptual isolation of notions like supply and demand, and insists on remaining an 'ecumenical' science.

Thus it is not sociological research which will introduce supply and demand as the criterion of preaching or provision: if anything it is ecclesiastical administration and bureaucracy which too easily succumbs to the false seductions of economics or of seeming economies. If Christians fear bureaucracy so do sociologists. But the fear of the sociologist is not of bureaucracy as such —he of all people does not use the word pejoratively—but he is concerned that the church bureaucracy shall not attempt to restrict the ecumenical sweep of his scientific interest, either by refusal to co-operate over delicate issues or by indifference to what appears to have no immediate pay-off. After all sociologists can hardly fail to recognize in the Roman Church (and those churches derived from it) the great inheritance of an imperial bureaucracy; and it is not unknown for bureaucrats to wish to restrict the range of enquiry. The same could apply in the Free Churches also. Paul Harrison has indicated the growth of the executive type even there: a process whereby old presbyter becomes Baptist organization man.[1]

This aspect of restriction by interested parties can relate to such relatively minor matters as the occasional suppression of ecclesiastical statistics. Or it may be that ecclesiastics only want the kind of information and analysis which will assist them in fairly limited objectives. To receive information about the optimum size of parishes in given areas is all very well, but an analysis of the social, as distinct from the theologically defined, role of the priest comes nearer the bone. For a sociologist to describe the empirical antecedents of the call of the Holy Ghost to the priestly vocation may be well-nigh improper.[2] Indeed, it is a general rule that the more the sociologist moves away from mere information about specific problems to an analysis which brings in the general function of churches and priesthoods the less welcome his presence is likely to be. There is a whole area

[1] P. Harrison: *Power and Authority in the Free Church Tradition*, Princeton University Press, 1959.

[2] Cf. E. Carlton: *The Probationer Minister: A Study among the English Baptists*, M.Sc.(Econ.) thesis, London 1965; and also 'The Predicament of the Baptist Minister', *New Society*, 7 January, 1965.

which is not precisely theology, but in which there is a particular ecclesiastical 'image' of how things take place, and here sociology and supposedly 'Christian' notions can easily appear to clash. Alternatively, the different status of sociological and theological accounts of events (like a 'call') may not be sufficiently clear to avoid tension.

This is why clergy and professional 'men of the church' often prefer psychoanalytic (or existential) images of the social world to sociological and structural ones. They raise a much smaller area of question and are in principle capable of assimilation to pastoralia. The psychoanalytic or therapeutic *persona* may even seem able to provide new clergy roles for old. That these are derived from an alien ideology and an alien priesthood need not matter over much. The new jargon has an advantage over that of theology in sounding like science. It would be a great linguistic improvement if recalcitrant individuals could be described as 'resisting' rather than sinning. Moreover, free rein for associational thinking as distinct from rigorous control also has its attractions.

Unfortunately clergy are not able to live in the fantasy world of the well-heeled therapist: they must come to grips with structures eventually. They need facts and they need intellectual rigour. But this factual aspect also excludes the kind of scholastic logic which is not grounded in empirical constraints. By the nature of their situation clergy can no more afford the chop-logic and learned ignorance of lawyers than they can the fantasy life of therapists. If they do they run the risk of knowing as little about the social anatomy of sin as judges know about the social anatomy of crime.

Facts are sacred, even to Christians. The greater likelihood of contemporary Christians recognizing this sanctity follows from the comparative non-availability of activities associated either with the legal or the therapeutic professions. The two roles of therapist and lawyer are themselves in extreme tension one with another, but between them they represent the old public and the new private ideology of a middle class which no longer needs priests to act as its spokesmen and comforters. The priest can rely neither on the legitimacy and legality of established modes of behaviour nor on the special sphere of the 'soul' defined as his preserve. He is being winkled out of the structure of legitimation and has potent, more acceptable rivals in the realm of the spirits. He may have no choice but to live in the real social world.

This critical semi-detached role requires sociological research as its very basis. It is quite different from that assimilation to other professions which is actually sought by some proponents of 'secularization'. Social workers for example (i.e. would-be therapists), do not provide a paradigm for the clergy since they in turn are becoming a well-organized pressure group with their own ideology and systems of professional defence. Clergy ought not to exchange the unhappy vocation of ideological spokesmen of the establishment for the professional pressure politics and entrenched psychologies of the self-vaunted medical and remedial role.[3]

The Church need not be entirely subordinated to any social actuality, or to any specialized vocation which partly depends for existence on masking what is really happening in society. Instead it is partly open for Christians to unmask the whole panoply of interested notions. Sociology is actually available as an instrument of this moral criticism. In such a perspective research is more than an interesting luxury or mere adjunct of efficiency; the facts can become the basis of 'judgement', not only in the secular sense of the word, but in the sense of the word of prophecy.

What then have I been trying to say? Firstly, that the Church need not model itself as in the past on public roles like that of lawyer, or, as more recently, on private roles like that of therapist. Nor does it need alien or alienated images of the social world for its own specific purposes; neither those provided by the science of economics nor those of the social work 'ideology'. It is bound to take all these into some account, of course, but what it most certainly needs is an image of its own social self and of

---

[3] Social work would frequently prove a most frustrating alternative to the professional ministry in view of the social worker's intense urge to professionalization and the inflated vocabulary accompanying that urge. As regards medical roles of all kinds the attempt to maintain social distance with clients or patients generally precludes decent personal relationships. In other words, if clergy wish to be pastors and friends, then they need to avoid any assimilation to professions which either have or seek to have a clinical ethos. In any case, why exchange one bureaucracy for another?

the society in which it operates.[4] And this is where research comes in.

What Happened Historically?

The first need is for research to find out what has happened historically and why. In this attempt Britain has a particular importance, along with France and Germany. As Engels pointed out over a century ago these three countries have a special interest as regards their social, political and philosophical development respectively. Britain acquires its central interest as the first industrial nation. But the French example indicates that we are not faced with a simple equation between industrialization and infidelity. Many of those areas which responded most willingly to the attack on the French Church by the Revolution were not even urban, and there are regions of intransigent rural atheism in France to this day. Thus the historical task is not simply to elucidate the impact of industrialization on religious attitudes and behaviour.

Nor, for that matter, is the impact of industrialization to be considered merely as the creation of the new internal proletariat of the working class. That is only the first half of the historical question, since the twentieth century increasingly illustrates not the simple confrontation of antagonistic classes, but the proliferation of status groupings and new occupations. The supposed dichotomy of nineteenth-century class is now partially overlaid by a burgeoning plurality of groups, roles and values held together by 'mass culture'. The history of religious institutions in relation to this plurality is as important as the aspect of straightforward class conflict. Indeed to concentrate overmuch on class is to ignore the fact that 'in industry and business white-collar workers are replacing the manual workers as the key group . . .'[5]; just as to discover belatedly the importance of the

---

[4] P. Rieff makes this general point in his *Freud the Moralist*, University Paperbacks 1965, p. 299, suggesting that clergy are at least guardians of 'symbols of remembrance' which preserve critical capacities absent from psychological cults. He points out that the religious dependency can check other dependencies: can one hope for more?

[5] M. Abrams, 'Social Trends and Electoral Behaviour', *British Journal of Sociology* 13 (4), Sept. 1962.

workplace is to ignore the significant home-centredness of advanced societies.

Yet, providing we do not allow ourselves to be bemused by the historical importance of the class cleavage and the centrality of work, then the advantages of historical study are considerable. There remain elements of continuity between our situation and that of the past. Basically these turn on the continuous differentiation of groups, professions and values. Just as the industrial revolution broke an integrated society into component halves, it then proceeded to a massive complication based on a quite new form of functional interdependence. This change remains with us, creating problems of integration at every level, from that of central government to the relation of home and workplace, and the psychological tensions derived from playing many roles or having to adapt them to new life situations.

Presumably what is needed is a local ecclesiastical history and religious social geography which will take this sociological perspective into account. There are a great many questions to be answered, especially concerning the relative weight of various factors, which were effective and which dependent. How great, for example, was the impact of the pew-rent system emphasized by Wickham in his study of Sheffield? One would like to know what particular elements in industrialization were crucial in alienating the working classes: was it basically the impersonality and scale of the new system? Again, what was the differential impact of the organization of different industries in various stages of their development? No one who has read Boulard's book on religious sociology can fail to be struck by (say) the impact of a line of quarries on religious practice in the otherwise devout area of Brittany.[6] What is it about stone-quarrying which has this effect?

Allied to these questions are those involving the response of the churches in terms of organization and evangelism. In the expanding town there is interest to be found in tracing the siting of various new daughter churches and the social as well as territorial catchment areas which they served. How have the churches

[6] For an interesting study showing a *positive* relation in an American locality between textile work and religious practice, cf. *American Journal of Sociology* 69, 1963.

coped with mobility in general, and under what circumstances have they been successful? In Britain for example, the 'religious' Welsh and Scots have accommodated themselves to English indifference on leaving their native countries, just as Bretons on the move accommodate to the indifference of Parisians. Yet in America the different churches have been lively centres for the maintenance of an immigrants' cultural identity, and East German migrants have been largely absorbed into Western German church life.[7]

A book by Birch on *Small Town Politics* shows the sort of approach that might be useful.[8] It demonstrates the relationship between politics, religion and economic forces in Glossop (Derbyshire) in the nineteenth century.

Birch shows how the mill-owners played an important part in the town's early development and welfare. Most of them built a mill, a church and a school, and their championship of the different churches was the hub of their other rivalries. They agreed of course about the need for discipline and good relations between masters and men, but their competition for communal influence was expressed through the churches and the political differences associated with them. Most small mill-owners were dissenting and along with local traders they sponsored a whole group of chapels, although certain Methodist chapels seceding in the 1840's had to be built by their working-class congregations.

All the dissenters to some extent accepted the successive leadership of two Unitarian families in the struggle against the Anglican and Tory families, who on their side sponsored some four new parish churches. This emulation, linked with the conflict between mill-owners and landowners, assisted local administration and the growth of facilities, such as schools and libraries and sports provision, with the Liberal-dissenting group characteristically claiming to lean more towards matters of the intellect. Eventually the system partially disintegrated when the Labour party drew off some of the more radical nonconformists and

---

[7] Partly to the extent that they have not achieved integration elsewhere, e.g. the socially weaker, single women and recipients of pensions; cf. T. Rendtdorff, *Die Soziale Struktur der Gemeinde*, Im Furche Verlag, Hamburg, 1959.

[8] A. H. Birch, *Small Town Politics*.

also some of the numerous local immigrants, notably on the issue of Home Rule for the Irish.

Such an account leaves us asking a number of questions. The continued connection between Liberalism and nonconformity suggests the sheer power of habit on personal identification. The curious maintenance of the Anglican-Conservative connection in the working class not only in Glossop but in the north-west generally (Catholic areas apart) raises queries about the original impact on working-class loyalty of Anglican support for the claims of operatives against mill-owners. One wonders further to what extent it is correct to see contemporary denominations here and elsewhere as representing fossilized social conflicts.

Women and Tradition; the Young and Change

Amongst the general social processes in industrial society there are two aspects of great importance for the churches. One is the activity of women in maintaining social continuity and in partly associating that continuity with the Church. The other is the activity of the young in breaking tradition and in partly associating that break with a severance of the umbilical cord of religious practice.

Let us first of all suggest ways in which the almost universal phenomenon of the religious and political conservatism of women may be studied. So far as this country is concerned we know that but for the feminine vote Labour government would have been continuous since the war. English religious practice passes largely through the distaff side. The factors involved are clearly complex and cumulative. We need to begin by asking how far the cluster of roles indicated by 'Küche, Kirche, und Kinder' is crucial: after all the separation of women from work as such is largely a nineteenth-century phenomenon. In peasant societies women do unpaid work alongside men.

Something must be put down to the fact that the impersonal conflicts of the industrial workplace are perceived as less central to the life of a woman than a man. The contagious political alienation of such conflicts is partly avoided. Women are able to retain a personalized image of the world more consonant with

Christian images. Presumably their biological functions structure their roles so as to make possible a response to the personal symbolism of Fatherhood, Motherhood and Sonship. Family duties bring them so close to the crises of birth, marriage and death that they necessarily make some minimum contacts with the Church and perhaps recognize that only the Church can remotely match in symbol and language what these crises mean.

Yet it seems paradoxical that women are so involved in an institution which is a central bastion of male superiority. It would be interesting to enquire about the psychology of the relationship between women and priests, particularly in Anglo-Catholicism. Perhaps it involves a purer eroticism, a less constricting dependency than that associated with the husband, particularly when he has become indifferent or is increasingly crude and distasteful. For many women the pursuit of good works is the only socially approved way of avoiding such a husband. Or it might be less fanciful to see the church as the female alternative to the public house because it provides a sorority of the women to offset the beery fraternal of the men? Even less fancifully one might just note that children are involved in church organizations, from choirs to cubs, and women are concerned with children. Maybe they also feel that a church connection is less dangerous than others for their offspring, as well as offering genteel possibilities.

At any rate it is clear that in our society, in spite of certain formal similarities between male and female education, the process of socialization moulds women for aesthetic and expressive attitudes, while men are prepared more for a world which is mechanical and instrumental. Whatever its origins, we need now to enquire how far the conditions ensuring this differentiation still obtain. If we find that women who go out to work often evidence a diminution of practice, is this merely a question of available time or a change in psychology? Presumably, as the working woman becomes more and more common, the level of female religious adherence will move towards that of men. Not entirely so of course, partly for the reasons mentioned above, but also because for many women work is less a career than a means of contact, and in any case is usually not in a factory *milieu* but in the personalized atmospheres of teaching, nursing and clerical work. Little group solidarity is ever achieved *vis-à-vis* authority in these professions and women often seem content to play out public versions of their private roles; looking after children or in some way enjoying secure subordination.

Margaret Stacey suggests that women's concern for the Church partly derives from their concern with the protection provided in a stable family. The woman stands to gain most from a stable family, and by extension comes to defend the stability of established institutions as such. Maybe. At any rate there is the inevitable corollary that high female representation in church affects the self-image of the clergyman in a rather deleterious way. One can imagine the impact on an American rabbi who finds himself increasingly a minder of Jewish wives while their husbands are at work. Something less extreme is the lot of most Christian clergy.

There is one further result which is worthy of note. It is the image of woman which clergy characteristically acquire. To listen to sermons one would never imagine that women were ever workers, professional people, or even secretaries. Always they appear as wives and mothers. And their relationship to husbands is nearly always represented as taking place in an aura of sniggering cosiness. The woman invariably uses her psychological skills to manipulate the practical man who is her half-conscious victim. Such views indicate the extent to which traditional views of womanhood find reinforcement within important sectors of the clerical perspective.

If women are the bearers and sufferers of tradition then young people are regarded as the source of possible changes. It is true that just as females stand higher than males on every index of religious activity so the younger stand lower than the older. One needs to remember however that figures for adolescents remain comparatively high until eighteen, and then drop, so that categories based on (say) ages sixteen to twenty may mislead. What we can only guess at is the extent to which this drop in practice and interest is consequent on new domestic and work roles which increasingly absorb those over eighteen and which then become less pressing from thirty-five to forty (or later).

It is not easy to assess the actual attrition of religious practice and attitude which continues to have effect as the young become middle-aged. Some attrition there almost certainly is, especially if we compare ratios of those confirmed over forty with those under forty, but a lot depends on what sociological (or indeed theological) weight one is prepared to rest on a relaxation of what (in some *milieux*) have been exceedingly conventional and meaningless rites of passage.

The myth of automatic youthful rebellion dies hard, and the conventional middle-aged are as much misled by anarchist marchers and much publicized teenage 'gangs' as the radical middle-class middle-aged are surprised by a youth that does not understand the leftish enthusiasms of the nineteen-thirties. Nor need we attribute to youth any special faculty for seeing through adult pretensions and hypocrisies. Discussion cannot be conducted in the spirit of 'Any Questions' pundits, declaring either that young people lack responsibility or that they are much abused idealists. By and large our educational system ensures that they are merely religiously and politically ignorant, and slightly more so than their elders. 20,000 Young Socialists do not make a radical generation, any more than 150,000 Young Conservatives make a political generation.

What may be true is simply this: that when two systems exist together, in a society where there is considerable mobility, the smaller of them (in this case the religious system or group of systems) is constantly eroded by the impact of the larger on its young. Whether a smaller group can maintain itself depends on developing separate institutions and the kind of ghetto psychology which also serves to inhibit mobility. Such a generalization would need to be stated with care, making a whole series of qualifications. Clearly the Roman Catholic community resists erosion much better than the Jewish community. But if current trends continue through processes of intermarriage etc., Jewry will be substantially diminished in Britain within a generation or so.

The general attitudes of young people in England have been studied from a variety of angles: moral sentiments, regard for parents, political awareness, sexual immorality, and so on, and in almost no respect do they emerge as adventurous and revolutionary. The researches by Musgrove, Schofield, Little and Abrams, and Eppel are remarkably consonant with each other.[9] They find little evidence of war between generations (apart from a resentment against school), and by implication this factor ought not to have any greater impact in the sphere of religion. However, there has been a certain amount of research by Goldman and Loukes into problems of maturation in relation to religious development which does suggest that the ages of fourteen to sixteen are not generally ages for commitment (even though such old-style 'conversions' as there are, occur more often in the adolescent years than later), and this has plain implications for the catechetical strategy of the churches.[10]

The young then are indifferent or accepting, fairly moral, friendly to parents, and concerned mainly about happiness in marriage and friendship, and in success at work: even the 'teen-age gangs' are not widespread and for that matter often not even genuine 'gangs'.[11] Nevertheless, one or two changes may be worth our attention, especially if we are anxious to study the diminution in the influence of Sunday Schools, of the uniformed organizations, and also the future of the youth clubs. It is true there has been no hysterical anxiety among social scientists to study Sunday Schools, but they have been institutions of first-rank importance and their decline is therefore interesting. Even smaller organizations, like the Church Lads' Brigade, once had fair influence, especially in the north-west.

The various youth cultures are moving down the age scale: and the age of leaving Sunday School is also earlier than it was.

[9] F. Musgrove, *Youth and the Social Order*, Routledge, 1964; P. Abrams and A. Little, 'The Young Voter in British Politics' and 'The Young Adult in British Politics', *British Journal of Sociology* 16 (2) and (4), June and Dec. 1965; F. M. Eppel, 'The Adolescent and Changing Moral Standards' in W. R. Niblett (ed.), *Moral Education in a Changing Society*, Faber, 1963; M. Schofield, *The Sexual Behaviour of Young People*, Longmans, 1965. See also F. M. Eppel and M. Eppel, *The Age of Uncertainty*, Routledge, 1966.

[10] R. Goldman, *Religious Thinking from Childhood to Adolescence*, Routledge, 1964. Perhaps it should be said that there is a strong case for making confirmation a rite giving a certain access to sacraments without any definition of a given degree of commitment or doctrinal rectitude. The sole subjective criterion would then be an understanding of the invitation involved in confirmation, together with a desire to accept it—a criterion indicating a minimum age of 12.

[11] Cf. D. Downes, *The Delinquent Solution*, Routledge, 1966.

E

Pop-star adulation is now almost a ten- to twelve-year-old phenomenon. How these youth cultures will affect church practice depends on the social strata in which they are operating, but there are one or two aspects of the kind of 'youth culture' most frequently before the televiewing adult eye which have implications for religious behaviour.

George Melly has pointed out a new ease of manner, a degree of narcissism which is illustrated in dancing, and an ability to exchange sexual roles without damage to personal standing.[12] Thus there is an autonomy symbolized in the new ease of manner, together with a certain sexual confusion. There are exceptions to this: at one end of the social scale the languid effeminacy of Oxford exquisites and at the other the aggressive brutalized masculinity of the 'rockers', but the middle area where it applies is large. Now, the older organizations of the churches existed to avoid just this: they emphasized discipline and sexual differentiation. Indeed they were somewhat philistine in the tradition of 'muscular Christianity' where men were all boys together. It is difficult to see how such organizations can continue to appeal widely, or how their present leaders, inducted into the old system, can hope to make much contact with young people. If there is no radical break at the level of opinion and conscious rebellion there does seem to be a quite widespread change of ethos. The sort of young male who will submit to some hearty good fun round the camp fire or find the scout gang show funny may not be with us much longer.

Perhaps the whole question of youthful autonomy or conduct by reference to peer groups should be considered in connection with a general crisis of authority: partly a rejection of patterns, partly a refusal to set examples. This crisis occurs in the universities and in social contexts quite apart from the churches, but in these other areas concrete rewards can be offered for compliance. This only raises the pressure to express independence of adults in any sphere where such rewards are not available, and if adults can be found who are sensitive with respect to religion (like clergymen) or who use it as coextensive with obedience (like schoolteachers) then young people will be happy to make a show

12 G. Melly, 'Gesture Goes Classless', *New Society*, 17 June 1965.

of irreligious independence.[13] The Boy Scout movement tried
to meet these tendencies early in the century by the notions of
example, leadership and even hero-worship. Nowadays however,
'heroes' are always of the same adolescent age and set patterns
only in the field of taste and fashion. Otherwise they are themselves symbols of autonomy: emphatically they are not
exemplars of disciplined endeavour. Like their fans they are
content to be rather than to do: they prescribe roles, not goals.
The unfortunate assimilation of Christ as 'hero, guide and friend'
or as elder brother to the prefects' concept of social order found
in the uniformed organizations only involves the churches
further in the erosion of these types of authority.

Investigation of all these trends may be undertaken in a variety
of ways: at the level of youth club statistics, by participant observation in youth groups, by sample questionnaires and so on. But
I would like to mention an approach adopted by my wife since
it involves a break with the 'experimental' norms of most contemporary social psychology.[14] It is assumed that to be scientific
one must isolate the relevant variable and this means that the
area of approved interest is restricted and the time scale of
observation drastically reduced. But on-going groups continue
for years and will not submit to any rigorous isolation of variables without ceasing to be themselves. Something needs to be
done in terms of a social psychological observation of the natural
history of various types of youth grouping over their particular
adolescent 'generation', generally four to five years. Only American gangs have really been investigated in this way.

When the particular field is that of the church one must ask

[13] Mr Alan Shelston has suggested to me a parallel type of process occurring
at more mature years among some intellectuals. The feelings of release associated with Marxism or Freudianism encounter a degree of structural recalcitrance which progressively disenchants their devotees, and this renders all the
more compulsive the need to express 'freedom' in those areas where limitation
appears less obvious: religion and (possibly) art. So the argument runs thus:
Marxist economics and prophetic sociology may be largely irrelevant and
Freudian therapy may be bogus, but at least Marx and Freud were right about
God. Whatever else happens in this wicked world we can at least be certain the
everlasting arms are not there. Faith inverted.
[14] Bernice Martin, 'A Case Study of Informal Adolescent Interaction in Relation to the Formal Structure of an Anglican Church' (privately circulated: to
be printed in *Social Compass*).

what relation exists between the declared formal aims and structure of the group and its informal structure and motivation. One must study the life-span of a group, its nuclei, the style and circumstances of differential recruitment, the formal and informal methods of excluding certain types of personality or social background, the distribution of roles, patterns of authority, which persons associated with whom on what basis, and so on. Clearly a great deal can be learnt by observing what factors led to a break-up: geographical and social mobility, marriage, college, or whatever. The results could be compared as between clubs e.g. of the religious evangelical type or the type based on general discussion and games. It might also be found that the survivors had certain common characteristics—even perhaps comprised persons who were misfits elsewhere and found the church their only possible group.

Micro-Processes: The Local Church

I would now like to turn to some questions which require answers concerning the social structures of congregations, in themselves and as related to structures in the community at large.

The word 'structure' is very frequent in sociological writing and, recently, in theological writing as well. Unfortunately it cannot be dispensed with, and is at least preferable to 'system' which suggests too high a degree of overall co-ordination and forethought. It also indicates that the sociological model of societies and churches is quite opposed to any alternative model of incidental collocations of individual atoms. This basic structure needs elucidating at every level of the churches' life, local, zonal and national.

The local church has been barely studied at all in England as a unit, apart from Conor Ward's study of a Roman Catholic parish *Priest and People*. Even this lays rather heavy stress on the formal structure. R. H. T. Thompson's examination of four parishes in Birmingham, *The Church's Understanding of Itself*, does precisely what its title suggests: it considers the way in which people view their membership. There is very little material comparable to Fichter's work in America, examining who is involved in concentric circles of parish participation from the nucleus to the periphery.

Even the establishment of layers of participation is not the elucidation of the formal and informal structures of congregations. The informal system is most important, since it frequently cuts across the apparent distribution of roles and authority. As in industry so in the church, the official organization has no necessary connection with what is established by practice. To give but one example, the formal system which established the independence of the local congregation was presumably not intended to create an informal system whereby wealthy elders substantially controlled the minister.

Obviously it would be of interest to consider the informal system of decision-making in local churches and how it is linked with formal structure. Who for example is elected to which posts in terms of age, sex and socio-economic status? Which groups indeed are available in terms of their self-perception and of time available to take up such posts?

A researcher is interested in what patterns of interaction occur in a church. Ways are available for actually charting these connections in the form of maps, establishing the *raison d'être* of particular hubs of interest, exclusive friendships and pockets of isolation. Nuclei are often of particular interest because they have a capacity to erode other persons not congruent with them and to repel newcomers in the sense that they are only slowly admitted through a kind of social probation. All those performing this ritual dance prescribe particular social circles, have certain anticipations of their own social magnetism and what is due in terms of the allocation of honorific positions. It is 'their' church, and, though ritual gestures of abnegation may be made, any minister or outsider who takes these expressions of humility and reluctance seriously will have to cope with rifts or hostility.

It needs no social scientist to point this out, but the process of freezing an initially flexible group of Christians into a tight immovable nucleus is important for the decline of local congregations and their capacity to repel new generations. Another result is that groups of Christians are extremely resistant to rationalization of church organization and buildings simply because their loyalties are so local and their primary concern so frequently with holding on to a post or a status which cannot be acquired again in a reorganized parish or circuit. The result can easily be the successful constriction of the active minister, whose loyalty is often to a wider church, and who can hardly regard the nuclei as ends in themselves.

Hence one finds local 'ideologies' framed precisely to express resentment at ministerial interference, even in such minor matters as adjustment of service times. If a person informally recognized as a 'key' figure fails to receive consultation the explosion may take on the air of grand questions of principle or be channelled into what are strictly quite unrelated issues. In this way major displays of aggression are transferred from the genuine issue to (say) the fact that a single light bulb has not been replaced for a fortnight. This displacement of tension, selection of symbolic battlefields, and the curious religious language used either by the combatants or eventually invoked in the strategy of reintegration is familiar to all who have attended church meetings. Ministers in particular need to acquire remarkable skills in waiting for the right moment to perform the verbal judo which catches the recalcitrant member on the wrong theological foot or which distributes just the right amount of psychic reward to prevent a grinding sense of corporate ingratitude for services rendered.

Malcolm Calley in his study of Pentecostalists gives examples of these techniques of masking conflicts. If a new leader is arising in a congregation the minister will preach a sermon which refers to precisely those means which the interloper is using to establish himself. (Conceivably he might preach on the theme of Absalom's treachery towards David.) The person referred to will then defend himself by speaking in tongues and giving a testimony which implicitly replies to the charges. The interesting point of these exchanges is that unless they occur fairly regularly the congregation may begin to melt away. It actually enjoys such verbal battles veiled in the language of Canaan, and these serve as a focus of interest and a release of feeling.[15]

[15] M. J. C. Calley, *God's People*, Oxford University Press, 1966. The bibliography (pp. 170-173) is helpful. Cf. also E. Allo Isichei's article on decision-making amongst nineteenth-century Friends, *Archives de Sociologie des Religions* 19, Jan.-June 1965, for an approach which could be used on contemporary material.

Macro-Processes: Ecclesiastical Politics

This perhaps is the raw material of observant novelists, but there is a wider zonal and national structure in the administrative machinery of the church, including the ecclesiastical civil service. There is a potential science of ecclesiastical administration which could actually draw on work done on civil service morale, types of industrial organization, the appropriate units of government and so on.[16] Here again one encounters the coercive vocabulary utilized to smooth the path of bureaucratic decisions, the paradigm case being 'it seemed good to the Holy Spirit and to us'. Younger clergy can usually be manipulated in this way, because they may still not know the rules of the verbal game. The game is not in itself of course reprehensible, and may be preferable to the exercise of direct authority, just as 'conscience' is generally preferable to violent coercion.

The deliverances of the bureaucracy on important matters, especially political issues, cannot very well avoid specialized language. The one necessary virtue is an appearance of firmness which masks any amount of internal flexibility. Each word by being pared down in this way or that can cumulatively alter the sense until it is substantially reversed. This ability can be exercised on articles of faith and it is useful for opening theological backdoors in awkward situations: 'You know, the church never really said X, which was a hostile gloss imposed by Y.' One can actually come to admire this ambidexterity which has the grace to recognize its own practice under the phrase 'economy of truth'. A fascinating example is found in Roman Catholic decisions on conscientious objection which broadly say that a man must always obey his own conscience and the call of the state. Even more instructive are the varied verbal and practical solutions to the current dilemma over artificial family limitation as posed by *Casti Connubii*: clearly the object must be simultaneously to preserve the magisterium of the Roman Church, prevent the

---

[16] I have in mind the sort of work done by P. Rudge on church organization (Ph.D., Leeds, 1966) and sociological considerations affecting administrative size etc. advanced by members of the William Temple Association in their evidence to the Archbishop's Commission on London and south-east England. Cf. M. Hewitt, 'Administrative Reform in the Church and Religious Sociology' in *Social and Economic Administration*, Exeter University, Jan. 1967.

exodus and hypocrisy of those who reject the teaching, and avoid an explosion among individuals who have suffered by their obedient orthodoxy.

Of course, this legal and linguistic skill is specially necessary where the church has close links with the state and is widely influential in a given society. The actual process of church-state integration or accommodation would be interesting: somehow we lack a sociological discussion of ecclesiastical politics. What, for example, are the media of communication; what role is played by the recruitment of political and ecclesiastical *élites* from identical strata? Nobody needs an analysis in the *Economist* to tell them that English bishops share a uniform social background with judges, military leaders and even commercial magnates, in spite of increasing recruitment of minor clergy from lower social strata.[17]

Still, there remains an interest in indicating just those points at which ecclesiastics may take issue with the political executive. For example Archbishop Fisher showed distinct uneasiness over Cyprus, and Archbishop Ramsey has been remarkably forthright over Rhodesia, 'misunderstanding' quite apart. The episcopal sensitivity to these issues reflects a certain ecumenical and missionary awareness in churchmen not available to secular politicians. One doubts if any Labour pioneer foresaw the day when the voice of black Africa against a settler minority would be the heir of the chair of St Augustine, to the embarrassment of the then Labour government. Certainly the process by which bishops have largely shifted to the liberal 'left' on issues like homosexuality, capital punishment and so on is an interesting one.

This shift has generated a distinct uneasiness amongst other sections of the *élite* groups which have not participated in it. Their conception of the episcopal and clerical role is solely that of legitimation, and they are deeply disturbed by discrepant behaviour. Once again, the language used is an index of a

---

[17] *The Economist*, 20 Oct. 1956. For careful contemporary analyses of clergy recruitment cf. A. P. M. Coxon, *A Sociological Study of the Social Recruitment, Selection and Professional Socialization of Anglican Ordinands* (with an extensive bibliography), Ph.D. thesis, Leeds, 1965; and D. H. J. Morgan, *The Social and Educational Backgrounds of English Diocesan Bishops of the Church of England, 1860-1960*, Ph.D. thesis, Manchester.

structure now under strain: ecclesiastical cobblers are told to stick to their lasts, and churchmen are then embarrassed to find causes about which they have grave reservations brought firmly under the sacred umbrella of 'our Christian heritage'. Actually there is a curious consensus in our society about this: most people feel that religious functionaries should not speak outside a given range of agreed humane issues.[18] Anyone who cares to document the reaction of politicians and others to those who step outside this arena has to work a richly comic vein of material.

The Demographic Context

The last field of research which I want to suggest is ecclesiastical statistics. Statistics about the church are already carefully collected, somewhat to the irritation of clergy, but there is no provision for them to be set in a relevant demographic context. Without this context the complicated task of interpretation cannot even begin.

I might give two examples which indicate the kind of factors which require attention. Firstly the rise and fall of 1955-1964 figures for confirmation in the Anglican Church occasioned considerable comment, none of which could be properly based until the figures were systematically related to the comparable pyramid for live births per 1,000 during the years 1944-1951. In fact most of this comment proceeded as if the actual 'availability' of bodies was not a relevant consideration. Secondly, quite mechanical factors can affect rates which have absolutely no connection with the effectiveness or 'appeal' of Anglican ministrations. The happy circumstance whereby more boys survive infancy than used to be the case means that the ratio of the sexes to each other has altered at the period of adolescence. This affects the proportions confirmed simply because larger proportions of girls are confirmed than boys. One need not suppose the impact of this factor other than marginal, but when combined with the impact of migrant populations etc., it is one item in an overall explanation.

---

[18] Mass Observation's *Puzzled People* provides illuminating material on reactions to statements by episcopal dignitaries. At a different level the author still relishes the outraged comment aroused when an Anglican vicar in Richmond tried to secure local housing for lower income groups and found himself impelled to stand for the council.

E*

The point about migration has already been made, but it is worth saying again that parts of England are already virtual Danelaw so far as native English are concerned. One cannot talk about proportions of the population baptized at Anglican fonts as if the one million Irish-born now in England had suddenly come within the Anglican purview by simply leaving the shores of Bantry Bay. Nor is it merely a matter of gross numbers but of their characteristics by age and sex and the consequences which these have for fertility at given periods of time.

The interesting complications of this study are illustrated by a quite recent controversy concerning the diocese of Ely in which it was suggested that church life in Ely was 'coming to a stop'. Now, so far as confirmation is at issue, the diocese stood only a little below the average for all dioceses in the two provinces of York and Canterbury with regard to the drop in candidates from 1961-1964. Even so, this did not necessarily dispose of the charge. It needed to be shown that births in Ely a decade or so previous had followed the national curve, and that no significant migrations of adolescent persons had occurred across diocesan boundaries. This done, there was a still more general question as to whether a rural diocese like Ely 'ought' to resemble the small group of rural dioceses which for unexplained reasons succeeded in largely defying the decline of numbers in the relevant age groups.

Plainly this would necessitate a full-scale examination of confirmation rates over time in all dioceses, taking all factors of population movement and births into account, as well as concentrations of public schools in given areas. Almost nobody proposed such an examination or even a preliminary survey of evidence, and my own attempts to secure such a survey were effectively squashed by refusal to publish my comments in the 'Church Times'. Yet it must be said that any comment not based in this way is quite useless, and that the sort of argument that immediately sets down a particular statistic as showing the results of 'South Bank religion' or even the inevitability of 'secularization' is an abuse of discussion.

One rather different area of ecclesiastical statistics might be that of the 'submerged constituencies' of different religious bodies with respect to their socio-economic characteristics and patterns of lapse. National polls have considerable information here, and there is also the kind of local investigation undertaken by Dr Pickering in a couple of northern towns. These at least indicate the unimportance to be assigned to intellectual difficulties (or, on the other side, to conversion), and the great importance of leaving school and the arrival of children.

This whole area: interfaith marriage, comparative fertility of those with high religious practice, the impact of an ageing population on church-going etc., offers a fascinating field, not the least because it brings into relief one of the prime problems of social statistics: the subjective meaning attached to a given rite by those who compose (or cease to compose) a group of statistical quantities, and how far the actual weight laid by church definition on given practices should be allowed to count. After all, if baptism has always been largely a matter of social rite plus superstition then our interpretation of changes raises a first-class intellectual problem. What *is* to count as 'pure religion and true'?

Concluding Unscientific Postscript

A careless reader of the preceding pages might have concluded that a sociologist (or at least this sociologist) is a pessimist and a determinist, with an irritated, cynical, and suspicious attitude towards whatever the bulk of humanity holds most dear. It seems that sociology is practically committed to the principle that nothing is ever what it appears to be and that nothing is sacred. Furthermore this pervasive contrast between appearance and reality apparently leads to a schizoid vision, a way of looking at the world from several different and even contradictory perspectives. These points are worth taking up one by one.

Most sociologists are not determinists. They merely assume certain stabilities and regularities without which social life would be impossible. All social organization must depend on anticipations and predictions, ranging from the likelihood of transport workers performing certain daily functions to the characterological consistency of people assigned to certain roles or positions of authority. Any genuine freedom depends on the wide dominion of hierarchies of habit.

If societies change they do so in accordance with particular rules and if we plan to change them we must plan within these rules. We can be sceptical about certain rules (the so-called laws of supply and demand, for example) but we are sceptical about rules *as such* only at our peril. Sociologists are conscious of these limitations on action and their mode of thinking can actually be described as an analysis of limits. Yet they also stress the freedoms which can be exercised within these limits, and are anxious to explode purely bogus rules which the custodians and beneficiaries of current social organization are anxious to elevate to the status of facts of nature. Society is bound by so many such bogus rules that the net impact of sociology cannot be other than liberating.

Since this is the case it is odd that sociologists should be viewed as threatening human dignity and autonomy when (say) an industrialist defending his 'share of the cake' on the basis of immutable facts and economic laws is not. For various reasons we have been conditioned to the one set of bogus rules and not conditioned enough to the rules which are genuine. (This itself is something of a social rule : that our images of social activity are systematically distorted by socialization and by the resistance of education systems to sociological awareness.) Rather curiously we believe that our political and religious attachments have a special autonomy and we think that a minor mistake by a pollster is somehow a vindication of that autonomy. We *talk* as if we didn't *know* that people of a given occupational ethos and living in a particular area have a specific likelihood of voting for party X as against party Y and that this is based on their fundamental social identifications.

Sociology merely assumes those stabilities whereby people on the average act and think in accordance with certain long-term social identifications and roles, both in politics and religion. We know that the floating voter in politics is not the paradigm of the free man : he is either at the meeting point of diverse pressures or the type of person who knows least about the issues. Freedom is not an unpredictable wobble. But this is not to assimilate persons to roles. Indeed to see the social world in terms of roles is to see these as in some sense acquired and therefore within limits dispensable. Let me illustrate.

The sociologist never uses sentences like 'A woman's place is in the home' or 'Women are irrational'. Such statements are genuinely deterministic (with ethical overtones of course) and actually avoid stating the conditions under which they may be more or less true. A sociological viewpoint would rather emphasize the psychological consequences, in terms of feminine capacity for rational decisions and attitudes, of confining and defining a woman's 'place' in a particular way. This opens up the possibility of varying the role, providing alternative possibilities, and observing the psychological consequences, as well as the effects of opening up these possibilities on the web of social relations in which roles are embedded.

The same flexibility holds with regard to the kinds of social avocations which are supposed to follow necessarily from the biological differentia of intellectual 'gifts'. Without doubt such differentia exist, but they partly depend for their quality and for the realization of their potential on the perspectives available from particular social statuses. Indeed the whole notion of a continuum of ability based on the kind of criteria appropriate to crossword puzzles is the nearest thing extant to a sin against the Holy Ghost. Intelligence only exists 'in action', i.e. in relation to a role, and the fact that, for example, creative scientists do not have especially high I.Q.'s tells us more about the intelligence of the testers than the I.Q.'s of the scientists.

These are just two incidental examples where sociology is in direct contrast to the more extreme kinds of social determinism rooted in biology; but it is also in contrast to the determinism which misuses the vocabulary of 'human nature'. Comparative study of cultural variation cannot help but produce some preliminary scepticism about this 'nature'. The main characteristic of 'human nature' appears to be plasticity and flexibility: an argument for freedom, not determinism. All sentences which begin: 'You can't go against "human nature"' are suspect.

There is an even wider determinism to which sociology cannot be a party and it derives from concepts actually associated with the Church. Since this is the case it is odd that some churchmen are alarmed by the supposed determinism of social science when so many of their own presuppositions exhibit similar attitudes. They have constantly spoken as if a whole series of specific material or social events, say illness and war, were literally 'acts of

God'. So doing they have not only blasphemed but lowered the Christian faith to the level of the diseased vocabulary of insurance.

Indeed, the ecclesiastical analysts of limits, at least until very recently, employed deterministic presuppositions of an unusually rigid kind. They treated limits as simple permanencies, instead of analysing the conditions under which they were either highly likely, or capable of circumvention, or even of utilization. It is true of course that there is a parallel exaggeration on the other side by heretics and sectarians, insofar as these have anticipated what is genuinely impossible, or not possible at a particular time and period. Something is required which lies between the determinism of the Church and the fantastic expectation of the sectarian, and which is not the naïve individualistic optimism of liberal Christianity. Certainly the supposition that things are now as they were in the beginning and ever shall be needs to be placed in tension with the saying that mountains may be taken up and cast into the midst of the sea.

We can now turn to the accusation that sociology is a kind of systematic cynicism and its practitioners secular Blougrams. As a matter of fact most sociologists are alarmingly committed, including the present writer, but they are happy in that their commitments do not permit them to accept resonant social fictions very easily. They do not *accept* them but they are not exactly *surprised* by them either. The 'cynicism' of the sociologist does not approximate to the frustration experienced by those rationalists who are constantly amazed by the persistence of irrational nonsense. The social function of nonsense is too clear to give cause for amazement. I would like to give two examples, which may illuminate the sociological position.

The first is very simple and is borrowed from some comments made by J. Clyde Mitchell about the 'function' of certain beliefs in maintaining the collective morale of a ruling settler minority initially exposed to democratic notions. He mentions two beliefs: one about the tribal chiefs being the genuine representatives of the black majority, and the other concerning the true originators of the magnificent ruins at Zimbambwe and elsewhere. Both these questions are testable and no exposition is required either of the results of such tests or of the attitude taken by Rhodesians to them. Nor does it need a sociologist to show the function of these false beliefs in settler ideology. Presumably no cynicism is involved in casting doubt on the validity of this kind of belief.

The second example is more complex. About a decade ago Edward Shils and Michael Young were involved in controversy with Norman Birnbaum over the meaning of the British Coronation. Birnbaum was extremely sceptical about any suggestion that the 'tawdry' gew-gaws of that ceremony represented a reaffirmation of some (assumed) system of common values, stretching back to the roots of 'Western' civilization in the succession of Solomon and Charlemagne. Now, the point about its meaning for observers was testable, since moral consensus is open to examination, but the wider points about the continuity of tradition and so on are *not* really testable and words like 'tawdry' are clearly loaded. Nevertheless this loading does not spring from cynicism but from a commitment, and this is the essential point. Such commitment to a social reality which symbolism disguises rather than expresses has something in common with Carlyle in *Sartor Resartus*: and no one could reasonably accuse Carlyle of cynicism.

Sociologists are simply subject to double vision based on the contrast between meaning and function. They cannot but be chronically suspicious of all the solemn paraphernalia of patriotism, the puppetry of law, the phraseology of religion, when these act socially as instruments of cohesion and domination. This is not to say that some cohesion and some degree of authority are dispensable, but simply that the ontological and other pretensions of their guardian concepts must be subject to severe scepticism.

On the other hand, the sociologist cannot be a utopian, and this means recognizing the way in which his commitments may empirically interfere with his own sociological statements, even though they do not enter into the logical status of the science which he practices. It also means a suspicion of 'openness' when this is prescribed either as a precondition of 'authentic' social living or of the church being its true self. To see the 'social truth' is not to prescribe existential 'authenticity' as a way out. Indeed, it is to see how people *depend* upon their roles, institutions, and social fictions for their being and their sanity. To that extent the schizoid condition of the social scientist is a form of insanity when viewed from the perspectives and norms of the society itself.

Complete 'openness' is not authenticity but a social vacuum. Yet to expose himself to certain forms of open vision is at least one aspect of the sociologist's role. This is why he may find that he must write about the Church as he does, holding nothing sacred except the open vision. This indeed is *his* form of existential freedom: 'Here I stand; I can no other.'

SELECT BIBLIOGRAPHY

This Bibliography is restricted to works on religion in Britain which have a sociological emphasis. It makes no effort to be comprehensive as regards the social history of religion. A full guide to community studies exists in R. Frankenberg's *Communities in Britain* (Pelican, 1966). A Bibliography dealing with wider aspects of the sociology of religion is to be found in *Religion in Secular Society* by Bryan Wilson (Watts, 1966). Useful readers have been edited by J. Milton Yinger (*Religion, Society and the Individual*, Macmillan, New York, 1961) and L. S. Schneider (*Religion, Culture and Society*, Wiley, New York, 1964).

Administrative Studies

M. Hewitt, 'Church Administration and Religious Sociology', *Social and Economic Administration*, Exeter University, Jan. 1967

M. Smart, *The Southwark Borough Survey*, 1966, esp. Part 2, obtainable from John Marshall Hall, Blackfriars, London EC

M. Smart et al. (William Temple Association), Evidence before the Archbishop's Commission on London and the South-East, 1966

B. Woolaston, *Report on the Church Situation in the Eight New Towns of the London Ring*, 1966, obtainable from the Parish Office, St Mary's, Woolwich, SE 18

Community and Related Studies

H. E. Bracey, *English Rural Life*, Routledge, 1959

T. Brennan, E. W. Cooney and M. Pollins, *Social Change in South-West Wales*, Watts, 1959

A. H. Birch, *Small Town Politics*, Oxford University Press, 1959

D. Caradog Jones, *Social Survey of Merseyside*, University of Liverpool Press and Hodder and Stoughton, 1934, vol. 3

T. Cauter and J. S. Downham, *The Communication of Ideas*, Chatto and Windus, 1954

I. Emmett, *A North Wales Village*, Routledge, 1964, esp. ch. 7

A. Geddes, *The Isle of Lewis and Harris*, Edinburgh University Press, 1955 (two chapters on religion)

T. Harrisson, *Britain Revisited*, Gollancz, 1961

E. Jones, 'The Distribution and Segregation of Roman Catholics in Belfast', *Sociological Review* 4 (2), Dec. 1956

E. W. Martin, *The Shearers and the Shorn*, Routledge, 1965

H. A. Mess, *Industrial Tyneside*, Ernest Benn, 1928 (section on religion)

T. M. Owen, 'The "Communion Season" and Presbyterianism in a Hebridean Community', *Gwerin* 1 (2), 1956

A. Rees, *Life in a Welsh Countryside*, University of Wales Press, Cardiff, 1950

A. Rees and E. Davies (eds.), *Welsh Rural Communities*, University of Wales Press, Cardiff, 1960

K. C. Rosser and C. C. Stacey, *The Family and Social Change*, Routledge, 1965

M. Stacey, *Tradition and Change: a Study of Banbury*, Oxford University Press, 1960 (chapter on religion)

E. R. Wickham, *Church and People in an Industrial City*, Lutterworth, 1957

W. M. Williams, *Gosforth: the Sociology of an English Village*, Routledge, 1956, esp. ch. 10

Sheffield Renewal Group, *Sheffield Report of Working-class Communities*, 1964, unpublished

Rural Methodism, Commission's Report to the 1958 Conference, Epworth, 1958

Sects, Secessions, Specialized Groupings

M. J. C. Calley, *God's People*, Oxford University Press, 1965

J. H. Chamberlayne, 'From Sect to Church in British Methodism', *British Journal of Sociology* 15 (2), 1964

C. Driver, *A Future for the Free Churches?*, SCM Press, 1962

E. A. Isichei, 'From Sect to Denomination among English Quakers', *British Journal of Sociology* 15 (3), 1964

A. Kiev, 'Psychotherapeutic Aspects of Pentecostal Sects among West Indian Immigrants to England', *British Journal of Sociology* 15 (2), 1964

A. A. MacLaren, Research into nineteenth-century religious secessions in Aberdeen, Department of Political Economy, Aberdeen (in progress)

D. A. Martin, 'The Denomination', *British Journal of Sociology* 13 (2), 1962

R. Robertson, 'Salvationism's Centenary', *New Society*, 2 July 1965

B. R. Wilson, *Sects and Society*, Heinemann, 1961

B. R. Wilson (ed.), *Patterns of Sectarianism: Ideology and Organization*, Heinemann, 1967

Demographic, Statistical and Survey Materials

ABC Television, *Television and Religion*, University of London Press, 1965

R. R. Alford, *Party and Society*, Rand McNally, Chicago, 1963

M. Argyle, *Religious Behaviour*, Routledge, 1959

BBC Audience Research Group: Listening figures for religious broadcasts and ratings with comments by audience panels

'The Audience for Meeting Point, Autumn 1958' (UR/59/1)

'The Audience for Sunday Morning Programmes on the Light, 1960' (LR/60/1535)

J. Brothers, 'Religion in the British Universities', *Archives de Sociologie des Religions* 18, July-Dec. 1964

K. A. Busia, *Urban Churches in Britain*, Lutterworth, 1966

D. Butler and collaborators, *Election Studies* (with material on religion of politicians), Macmillan, 1952 and onwards

D. Clark, *Survey of Anglicans and Methodists in Four Towns*, Epworth, 1965

P. Dodd et al., *Census of Attendance in Anglican Churches in Rotherham*, Steel, Peech and Tozer, Rotherham, 1964

F. M. and M. Eppel, *The Age of Uncertainty*, Routledge, 1966

D. V. Glass, 'Religious Adherence, Habits and Practice in Relation to General Demographic Characteristics of a Random, Stratified Sample of Londoners' (LSE); privately available; part of the Third London Survey

R. Goldstein, 'Types de Comportment Religieuse et Cadres Sociaux dans deux Paroisses Catholiques Anglaises', *Revue Française de Sociologie* 6 (1), 1965, pp. 58-67

G. Gorer, *Exploring English Character*, Cresset Press, 1955

C. C. Harris, 'Church, Chapel and the Welsh', *New Society*, 21 Feb. 1963

J. Highet, *The Churches in Scotland Today*, Jackson, Glasgow, 1950

The Scottish Churches, Skeffington, 1950

'The Protestant Churches in Scotland', *Archives de Sociologie des Religions* 8, July-Dec. 1959

'Scottish Religious Adherence', *British Journal of Sociology* 4(2), 1953

Ch. 20 on 'The Churches' in *The City of Glasgow*, ed. J. Cunnison and J. B. S. Gilfillan, Collins, 1958

J. A. Jackson, Opinion Enquiry on 'Church, Society and Social Change', 1965, obtainable from the University of East Anglia, Norwich

H. Loukes, *Teenage Religion*, SCM Press, 1961

R. D. Macleod, 'Church Statistics for England', *Hibbert Journal* 46, July 1948

D. A. Martin, 'Sociological Aspects of Confirmation', in a symposium published by SPCK, 1967

Mass Observation, *Puzzled People*, Gollancz, 1948

F. T. Pagden, *Analysis of Church Membership in Parts of the Liverpool District*, unpublished, 1964-65

W. S. F. Pickering (ed.), *Anglican-Methodist Relations*, Darton, Longman and Todd, 1961

W. S. F. Pickering, 'Religious Movements of Church Members in Two Working-class Towns in England', *Archives de Sociologie des Religions* 11, Jan.-June 1961
A Study of the Rev. Dr Abraham Hume, University of Durham, unpublished

P. K. Poppleton and G. W. Pilkington, 'The Measurement of Religious Attitudes in a University Population', *British Journal of Social and Clinical Psychology* 2, 1963

B. S. Rowntree and B. R. Lavers, *English Life and Leisure*, Longmans, 1951

C. T. Sandford and S. Griffin, 'Religious Belief and Attendance at a College of Science and Technology', *Church Quarterly Review* 166, July-Sept. 1965

R. Silvey, *Religious Broadcasts and the Public*, BBC Audience Research Department, 1955

A. E. C. W. Spencer, *The Post-war Growth of the Catholic Child Population of England and Wales*, Catholic Education (a handbook), 1961

R. Stark, 'Class, Radicalism and Religious Involvement', *American Sociological Review* 29 (5), Oct. 1964

B. Woolaston, *Membership Studies: St Mary's and St Andrew's, Woolwich; New Eltham Survey*, Feb. 1966 (cyclostyled); both obtainable from the Parish Office, St Mary's, Woolwich, SE 18

F. Zweig, *The Worker in an Affluent Society*, Heinemann, 1961, esp. § 29

General Discussions on the Place of Religion

N. Birnbaum, 'Monarchs and Sociologists', *Sociological Review* 3 (1), July 1955

L. Bright and S. Clements (eds.), *The Committed Church*, Darton, Longman and Todd, 1966

J. Brothers, 'Youth in the Changing Church', *New Life* 20 (1), 1964

R. A. Buchanan, 'Religion and the Working Classes', *Theology* 61, May 1958

M. P. Hall and N. Howes, *The Church in Social Work*, Routledge, 1965

J. D. Halloran and J. Brothers (eds.), *The Uses of Sociology*, Sheed and Ward, 1966, esp. chapter by A. E. C. W. Spencer

S. H. Mayor, 'The Religion of the British People', *Hibbert Journal* 59, Oct. 1960

G. F. Thomason, 'The Industrial Challenge to the Church', *Province*, Winter 1963

B. R. Wilson, *Religion in Secular Society*, Watts, 1966

M. Young and E. Shils, 'The Meaning of the Coronation', *Sociological Review* 1 (2), Dec. 1953

General Surveys

N. Birnbaum, 'Nuffield Conference on the Sociology of Religions', *Archives de Sociologie des Religions* 11, Jan.-July 1961
'La sociologie de la religion en Grand Bretagne', *Archives de Sociologie des Religions* 2, July-Dec. 1956

J. Brothers, 'Recent Developments in the Sociology of Religion in England and Wales', *Social Compass* 11 (3-4), 1964

J. Highet, 'Review of Socio-Religious Literature in Scotland', *Social Compass* 11 (3-4), 1964

M. J. Jackson, Bibliographical review: 'The Sociology of Religion', *The Technologist* 2 (3), 1965

D. A. Martin, J. A. Jackson and R. Moore, Papers on the Sociology of Religion originally given at the British Association, Sept. 1965, and printed in *Advancement of Science*, June 1966 (also in *The Listener* during June 1966)

D. Wainwright, *Religious Sociology* (Prism Pamphlet 7), Prism Publications, 1964

J. T. Wilkinson (ed.), *The London Quarterly and Holborn Review*, Jan. 1963 (an issue largely devoted to the sociology of religion)

Historical Background

C. Booth, *Life and Labour of the People in London*; Third Series: *Religious Influences*, 7 vols., Macmillan, 1902-3, esp. vol. 7

C. Cannon, 'The Influence of Religion on Educational Policy 1902-1944', *British Journal of Educational Studies* 12 (2), May 1964

D. B. Clark, *A Social History of the Christian Churches in Rugby*, 1964, unpublished; obtainable from 65 Station Road, Woodhouse, Sheffield

J. S. Cowan, *Church and People in a Cheshire Town*, a post-ordination essay, 19xx, unpublished; obtainable from Crewe Public Library

E. T. Davies, *Religion in the Industrial Revolution in South Wales*, University of Wales Press, Cardiff, 1965

C. Driver, 'The Nonconformist Conscience', *New Society*, 27 June 1963

D. Hankey, *A Student in Arms*, Melrose, 1919

A. Hume, Unique map showing the spiritual destitution of seventy-three great towns in England; specially printed for a Report of a Committee of the House of Lords, 1859
Remarks on the Census of Religious Worship (1851), with a map, 1860
Results of the Irish Census of 1861, Rivingtons, 1864

K. S. Inglis, *Churches and the Working Classes in Victorian England*, Routledge, 1963

'Patterns of Religious Worship in 1851', *Journal of Ecclesiastical History* 11 (1), April 1960

J. A. Jackson, 'The Irish in Britain', *Sociological Review* 10 (1), March 1962
The Irish in Britain, Routledge, 1963

M. J. Jackson, 'Charles Booth's *Life and Labour of the People in London*', *Theology* 64, Nov. 1961

J. Kennedy, 'On the Census Returns Respecting Congregational Worship', *Congregational Year Book*, 1855

J. A. Lesourd, 'La déchristianisation en Angleterre vers le milieu du XIXe siècle', *Cahiers d'histoire* 11 (3), 1964

Liverpool Daily Post, Religious censuses decennially from 1831 to 1912. See issue of 13 Dec. 1912 (reported in D. Caradog Jones, *A Social Survey of Merseyside*, 1934, vol. 3)

W. G. Lumley, 'The Statistics of the Roman Catholics in England and Wales', *Journal of the Statistical Society* 27, Sept. 1864

H. Mann, *Census of 1851* (C. 1690): Report on Religious Worship

A. A. MacLaren, 'Presbyterianism and the Working Class in a Mid-nineteenth-century City', to be published in the *Scottish National Review* during 1967

J. J. C. Probert, 'The Sociology of Cornish Methodism', *The Cornish Methodist History Association*, No. 8, 1964
Primitive Methodism in Cornwall, 1966, available from the author at 1 Penventon Road, Redruth

J. Rogues de Fursac, *Un mouvement mystique contemporain*, Paris, 1907 (on the 1904 Welsh Revival)

T. S. Simey, *Charles Booth*, Oxford University Press, 1960 (esp. the chapter on religion)

F. Tillyard, 'Distribution of the Free Churches in England', *Sociological Review* 27, 1935

E. H. Tindall, *The Wesleyan Methodist Atlas of England and Wales*, 1873 (available in archives of Epworth Press)

E. P. Thompson, *The Making of the British Working Class*, Gollancz, 1963; sections on Methodism

C. R. Williams, 'The Welsh Religious Revival 1904-05', *British Journal of Sociology* 13 (3), Sept. 1962

YMCA, *Report on the Army and Religion*, 1919

'Religious Census of Bristol', *Western Daily Press*, 2 Nov. 1881

Report of the Fifth Annual Meeting of the British Statistical Society, Nov. 1841

Parish Studies

J. Brothers, 'Two Views of the Parish', *The Furrow* 16 (8), 1965
Education, Social Change and Parish Membership', Conference Internationale de Sociologie Religieuse, 1962

'Grammar School versus Parish', *The Clergy Review* 48 (9), 1963
Church and School, Liverpool University Press, 1964
R. Goldstein, 'La minorité Catholique d'une petite ville industrielle anglaise', *Archives de Sociologie des Religions* 9, Jan.-June 1960
M. J. Jackson, 'Parish and Community Today', *Parish and People* 40, Epiphany 1964
'The Rural Church and the Sociology of Religion', *Church Quarterly Review* 164, Jan.-March 1963
'Church and City', *Church Quarterly Review* 162, Oct.-Dec. 1961
B. Martin, 'A Case Study of Informal Interaction in an Adolescent Group within a formal Anglican Structure', to be published in *Social Compass* during 1967
R. H. T. Thompson, *The Church's Understanding of Itself*, SCM Press, 1957
C. K. Ward, *Priest and People*, Liverpool University Press, 1961
'Some Aspects of the Social Structure of a Roman Catholic Parish', *Sociological Review* 6 (1), July 1958

Priesthood and Ministry

J. Brothers, 'Social Change and the Role of the Priest', *Social Compass* 10 (6), 1963
'The Priest's Role', *New Society*, 1 Oct. 1964
'Catholic Reflections on the Paul Report', *Heythrop Journal* 6 (1), 1965
E. Carlton, 'The Predicament of the Baptist Minister', *New Society*, 7 Jan. 1965
D. B. Clark, *Group Ministry*, Renewal Group Policy, Paper 1, 1965
'Six Types of City Ministry', *New Directions*, Dec. 1964
A. P. M. Coxon, 'Patterns of Occupational Recruitment: the Anglican Ministry', *Sociology*, Jan. 1967
'An Elite in the Making' (material on Clergy recruitment), *New Society*, 26 Nov. 1964
D. A. Martin, 'The Methodist Local Preacher', International Conference of Religious Sociology, Montreal, 1967
L. Paul, *The Deployment and Payment of the Clergy*, Church Information Office, 1964
L. Paul and B. Wilson, articles in *Theology* 68, Feb. 1965 and subsequent issues
J. Peart-Binns, collection of materials with special reference to the Ministry, available at 9 Tufton Street, London SW 1

Minorities

R. Allison, *An Enquiry into the Contact of Methodist Churches with the Coloured Immigrant, Manchester and Stockport District*, 1966

L. P. Gartner, 'From Jewish Immigrant to English Jew', *New Society*, 2 Sept. 1965

J. Gould and S. Esh (eds.), *Jewish Life in Modern Britain*, Routledge, 1964

C. S. Hill, *West Indian Migrants and the London Churches*, Oxford University Press, 1963

D. Mathew and I. Evans (eds.), *Catholicisme Anglais*, Editions du Cerf, Paris, 1958

Sheila Patterson, A study of migration to England (in progress)

Theses

J. Absalom, *Anglo-Catholicism: Ideology and Influence*, M. Phil., London (in progress)

M. Austin, *Church and People in Derby, 1824-1885*, M.A., Birmingham, presented Sept. 1966
Church and People in the Midlands, 1885-1965, Ph.D., Birmingham (in progress)

M. Bathis, *Local Preaching in the Methodist Church*, M.A., Leeds (in progress)

J. C. G. Binfield, *Nonconformity in the Eastern Counties, 1840-1885, with Reference to its Social Background*, Ph.D., Cambridge, 1965

L. Burton, *The Social Stratification of Two Methodist Churches in the Midlands*, Ph.D., London (External), 1967

E. Carlton, *The Baptist Probationer Minister*, M.Sc. (Econ), London, 1965

D. Carter, *Social and Political Influences of Bristol Churches, 1828-1914*, Bristol (in progress)

A. P. M. Coxon, *A Sociological Study of the Social Recruitment, Selection and Professional Socialization of Anglican Ordinands*, Ph.D., Leeds, 1965 (see further the bibliography to this thesis)

R. Currie, *Divisions and Reunions in Methodism*, D.Phil., Oxford, 1966

M. Daniel, *New Clergy in London: a Survey of Changing Attitudes and Self-images amongst a Sample of Clergy during the Ten Years after Ordination*, M.Phil., London, 1967

A. Dawson, *Attitudes to Morality in a Liverpool Area*, M.Sc., Liverpool, 1966

W. C. Dowling, Projected thesis on the Methodist Ministry since Union, London (30 Court Lane, SE 21)

J. Gay, *The Social Geography of Religion in Britain*, D.Phil., Oxford (in progress)

R. Goldstein, *Some Features of the Catholic Church in England: the Life of an Industrial Northern Parish*, Paris, 1958

J. Hickey, *The Origin and Growth of the Irish Community in Cardiff*, M.A., University of Wales (Cardiff), 1959

M. Hill, *The History and Structure of Anglican Religious Orders*, D.Phil., Oxford (in progress)

J. A. Jackson, *The Irish in London*, M.A., London, 1958

P. Jackson, *Industry and Religion in Port Talbot, 1750-1956*, M.A., University of Wales (Cardiff), 1957

D. H. J. Morgan, *The Social and Educational Background of English Diocesan Bishops of the Church of England, 1860-1960*, Ph.D., Manchester (partly summarized in the Paul Report, pp. 282-85)

G. K. Nelson, *Spiritualism in Britain*, Ph.D., London (External), 1967

W. S. F. Pickering, *The Place of Religion in the Social Structure of Two English Industrial Towns*, Ph.D., London, 1958

V. Pons, *Social Structure of a Hertfordshire Parish*, Ph.D., London, 1955 (esp. chapter on religion)

R. Ritson, *Church and Family: a Study in Anglican Methods of Teaching the Laity*, M.A., Liverpool (in progress)

D. R. Robertson, *Church and Class in Scotland*, Ph.D., Edinburgh, 1966

C. S. Rodd, *A Comparison of Attitudes to Social Questions between Three Church Groups and a Control Group of Non-churchgoers*, M.A., Birmingham (Handsworth College, Birmingham 20) (in progress)

P. Rudge, *Study of Ecclesiastical Administration with Special Reference to Organization Theory*, Ph.D., Leeds, 1966

S. Sharot, *Changing Values, Practices and Organization of English Jewry, especially in relation to the United Synagogue*, D.Phil., Oxford (in progress)

G. F. Thomason, *The Effects of Industrial Changes on Selected Communities in South Wales*, Ph.D., University of Wales (Cardiff), 1963

D. M. Thompson, *Religion in the East Midlands during the Nineteenth Century*, Ph.D., Cambridge (in progress)

K. A. Thompson, *Organizational Response of the Church of England to Social Change, with Special Reference to the Emergence of the Church Assembly*, D.Phil., Oxford (in progress)

R. Towler, *An Analysis of Occupational Choice and Theological Education*, Department of Social Studies, Leeds (in progress)

B. Turner, *Methodism in Leeds, 1914 to the Present Day*, Ph.D., Leeds (in progress)

P. Varney, *The Social Geography of South Norfolk with Special Reference to Religion*, M.A., Durham (in progress)

T. R. Warburton, *A Comparative Study of Minority Religious Groups: with Special Reference to Holiness and Related Movements in Britain in the Last Fifty Years*, Ph.D., London, 1966

J. Whitworth, *Religious Utopianism* (including Brüderhof in England), D.Phil., Oxford (in progress)

J. Wilson, *A Study of the British Israelites—a Case of Downward Social Mobility*, D.Phil., Oxford, 1965

B. Woolaston, *Church Arrangements in New Towns*, M.A., London (projected)

INDEX OF NAMES

INDEX OF SUBJECTS